NIGHT IN CAMP

The River and I

John G. Neihardt

Introduction to the Bison Books
edition by Timothy G. Anderson

UNIVERSITY OF NEBRASKA PRESS
LINCOLN AND LONDON

Introduction © 1997 by the University of Nebraska Press
Manufactured in the United States of America

⊛ The paper in this book meets the minimum requirements of
American National Standard for Information Sciences—Perma-
nence of Paper for Printed Library Materials, ANSI Z39.48-1984.

First Bison Books printing: 1968
First Bison Books printing of this edition: 1997
Most recent printing of this Bison Books edition indicated by the last
digit below:
10 9 8 7 6 5 4 3 2 1

Library of Congress Cataloging-in-Publication Data
Neihardt, John Gneisenau, 1881–1973.
The river and I / by John G. Neihardt; introduction to the Bison
Books edition by Timothy G. Anderson.
p. cm.
Previously published: Lincoln: University of Nebraska Press, 1992.
Includes bibliographical references (p.).
ISBN 0-8032-8372-5 (pa: alk. paper)
1. Missouri River—Description and travel.   2. Yellowstone River—
Description and travel.   3. Neihardt, John Gneisenau, 1881–1973—
Journeys—Missouri River.   I. Title.
[F598.N39   1997]
917.804'2—dc21
97-2250   CIP

Reprinted from the original 1910 edition by G. P. Putnam's Sons,
New York. Reprinted by arrangement with the John G. Neihardt
Trust.

To

MY MOTHER

INTRODUCTION

TIMOTHY G. ANDERSON

John G. Neihardt's *The River and I*, a book-length account of his 1908 descent of the Missouri River, is many things: It is part adventure story, a tale of three young men in an open boat battling headwinds and hunger to retrace the paths of heroes gone before; it is part travelogue, the young Plains poet in the first decade of his career awestruck before the transcendent beauty of the rich river valley; it is part autobiography, a chronicle of Neihardt's early boyhood and how his fear of the Missouri River turned to fondness.

But most importantly, *The River and I* is an outline, a plan— not yet fully formed—for an epic account of the settling of the West by an author so steeped in both the West and the classics that, writing only what he knew, he seemed destined to combine these two disparate influences to become the American Homer. If the Missouri River was the great road to the West, the pathway to its history, it was also Neihardt's route to his epic.

"I've been reading over *The River and I* after, oh, sixty years," Neihardt told an interviewer late in life, "and I was struck by the fact that the first chapter is called 'The River of an Unwritten Epic.' Well, I hadn't planned any epic cycle at that time. But all the way through that first chapter I'm pointing out that it's epic material."[1] In 1912 Neihardt began such an epic telling: *A Cycle of the West*, his life's work, chronicled the history of the fur trappers and the Indian wars from 1822 to 1890, in five volumes of epic poetry. "It must have been in the back of my head all the time,"

Neihardt said. "I was proving, as though someone had denied it, that there was epic material there."[2]

By 1908 Neihardt had tried his hand at editing a country weekly newspaper and reporting for a city daily, neither with much success. For Neihardt, just beginning to gain recognition as a lyric poet and short-story writer, *The River and I* was his first major prose work—and, some believe, his first writing of consequence.[3] It recalls his earliest years not as a time marked by poverty and the abandonment of the family by his father, which it was, but as a time of his monumental fascination with the larger-than-life Missouri River.

The book was commissioned as a series of articles for *Outing*, a magazine owned by a group of wealthy sportsmen and headed by the respected editor Caspar Whitney, a well-known traveler, hunter, explorer, and writer.[4] Whitney knew Neihardt through his poetry and short stories, and in fact, in March 1908 had sent Neihardt a copy of *A Bundle of Myrrh*, Neihardt's frank collection of short poems, with a request for an autograph.[5] In December 1908, shortly after Neihardt completed his Missouri River trip, *Outing* devoted twelve pages, plus two full-page illustrations, to "The Epic-Minded Scot," a Neihardt short story that depicts fur trapper Wallace McDonald in terms that could just as well have been used for Neihardt himself: "I could perhaps best describe him as epic-minded. He dreams large."[6] By 1909, however, Whitney and his partners had grown tired of the magazine business, and *Outing* was sold. Though some of the older contributors stayed, the younger, better-known writers left the magazine.[7]

Neihardt's series of articles ran instead in *Putnam's Monthly*, a literary magazine with a circulation of more than one hundred thousand, beginning in the December 1909 issue. Neihardt was not unknown to *Putnam's* readers either. A year earlier Jeanette Gilder, *Putnam's* editor, had mentioned in her popular column, "The Lounger," the two books Neihardt had thus far published, *A Bundle of Myrrh* and *The Lonesome Trail*, a collection of short stories. "Neither of these contained his first appeal to the reading public," she wrote. "*That* was made when he was but seventeen years old, and his long poem, *The Divine Enchantment*, was reviewed—and praised—as the work of a full-grown man, not of a lad in his middle teens." Then she brought readers up to date: "I understand that Mr. Neihardt is about to make a two-thousand-mile voyage down the Missouri in a house-boat, in the interest of *Outing*."[8]

The trip would be made by open boat, not by houseboat, and in the end, she would publish the series herself. But the assignment was otherwise accurate. In July 1908 Neihardt, then age twenty-seven, and two companions—William L. Jacobs, a photographer from Oakland, Nebraska, near Neihardt's home of Bancroft; and Chester Marshall, known in *The River and I* as "the Kid," a teenager who worked at the Bancroft depot—traveled to the headwaters of the Missouri River, at Fort Benton, Montana, to begin a trip down the river and, imaginatively, back in time. This book, the record of Neihardt's journey, is evidence of what the river meant to him and what he believed it meant to the history of the West.[9]

The Missouri River had fascinated John Neihardt since his childhood in Kansas City. "There I discovered the Missouri River," he once wrote, "which became to me what the ocean must have been to the young Greeks."[10] Like Mark Twain and his Mississippi River, or Walt Whitman and his ocean, or Henry David Thoreau and his Concord and Merrimack Rivers, or even Virgil and his Simois, Neihardt identified with—and would forever be identified with—the Missouri River. At age six, he first saw the river escape its banks. "We were standing on a blufftop in Kansas City, and the whole world beneath us, and far as we could see, was a chaos of wild waters," Neihardt remembered. "It was my second encounter with elemental grandeur; and what happened to me that day as I stood on the windy blufftop, holding fast to my father's forefinger for safety, did much to determine the direction of my lifelong striving."[11]

Despite his aborted attempts at journalism, Neihardt throughout his life relied on the skills of a reporter in researching his work. He knew the stories of the fur trappers from his reading and from listening to the old men talk on the Kansas City docks. Now, with a magazine commission, he could afford to experience for himself what the trappers, and Lewis and Clark and their Corps of Discovery before them, had experienced. If he was going to use the Missouri River in his writing, he needed to explore it himself, "to bind himself, across a hundred years of history, to the fur traders who had also shared a tender haunch around an open fire."[12] At this point, Neihardt likely considered the trip, in the most practical terms, as research for work in prose rather than poetry, and indeed, he makes use of it in some of his short stories.[13] But if he had not yet made the conscious decision to write the western epic, he is beginning to paint the background for *A Cycle of the West*. When he mentions mountain men Hugh Glass or Mike Fink, he is challenging himself to tell their story.

In the early 1900s America was not far removed from a time when its rivers had been roadways: to adventure, to a new world, to a new life. The country was led by an adventurer, President Theodore Roosevelt, and it was captivated by the outdoors, including its waterways. Early copies of *The River and I* carried five pages of advertisements in the back for other books in the "American Waterways" series, such as *The Story of the Chesapeake*, *The Romance of the Colorado River*, and *Narragansett Bay*. But Neihardt's title told readers they were going to get something extra with his book. It wasn't called *The Missouri River* or *The River West* or *The Pathway to Defeat and Glory*. Instead, his book had two subjects, set up equally in the title, *The River and I*, thereby promising readers insight not only into the Missouri River and its place in history but also into the writer himself, and introducing a theme that would carry through all his work: the balance between man and his universe.

Neihardt's first biographer wrote of Neihardt and the Missouri River: "What Neihardt loves possesses him."[14] Not until 1930, when he met Black Elk, the American Indian mystic who would tell him his life's story and about whom he would write his most famous book, *Black Elk Speaks*, would Neihardt find an influence as strong as the Missouri River. And it was clear to reviewers of the day, most of whom found the book lively and full of adventure, that Neihardt found joy in his journey from Fort Benton to Sioux City, Iowa.

"Poetry and charm would not be looked for by many in the mud of the Missouri River," wrote one reviewer. "Nevertheless Mr. John G. Neihardt, the Nebraska poet, has found inspiration in that turbid flood of waters for his volume of romance from real life."[15] Another wrote, "It's a mighty good thing when a man with a sense in him of the poetry of nature and of human life can write of such a phenomenon as the Missouri River in a fashion to bring out the big, epic implications of the theme. That's what John G. Neihardt, the Nebraska poet, does in his book, happily called *The River and I*."[16] *The Nation* called Neihardt "a cheerful philosopher" and added, "The author sees his world through rose-colored glasses; a balky engine, boiling rapids, sand-banks, mud-bars, head winds, hunger, cheerless days and nights, serve only to spur his enthusiasm, and to add a lustier zest to his song in praise of life in the open."[17]

Neihardt tells his story as though he were sitting with readers around a campfire. At one point he is philosophical and reflective, at the next, funny and exaggerated. Neihardt writes directly to readers and punctuates his tale with a "bully" and an exclamation point, and we can almost imagine him slapping his knee as he recounts the day's journey. It's almost as if he can see his readers' faces; when he finds he's getting too serious, he lightens the mood—but only after first making his point.

An epic tale, Neihardt believed, required an epic treatment, and modern readers may sometimes be puzzled by the grandiose language and the frequent Greek, Latin, and obscure literary references. But Neihardt loved the classics—he had excelled at Latin as a student and would eventually teach himself Greek—

and he cannot help but compare the travails of his mountain men to those of the ancient heroes. If some of his references are antiquated, his sense of humor is not. When he writes here of the Greek Agamemnon, "Today we should merely have a sensational trial, and hysterical scareheads in the newspaper," it's hard to believe that he hasn't been watching coverage of much more recent celebrity trials.

When Neihardt traveled the Missouri, only one dam had yet been built—at Black Eagle Falls—and he wasn't fond of that one. "The nature lovers may sympathize with Mr. Neihardt in his regret at the chaining of these huge natural forces," the editor of *Putnam's* wrote at the time, "but their utilization by the Great Falls Water-Power and Townsite Co. is one of the most important achievements of the day in the American industrial world."[18] Neihardt might be even unhappier with the situation today: the Army Corps of Engineers now has six dams between Fort Benton and Sioux City.

For Neihardt, the Missouri River was interwoven into the tapestries of his writing and of his life. Once, talking with a friend about the river, Neihardt said that upon his death he wanted his ashes strewn across it, "by way of expressing my lifelong devotion to that river."[19] The Missouri had always been a family affair—he was introduced to it by his father, and he dedicated this book to his mother—and after he died in November 1973, his daughters saw to it that his wish was fulfilled. Neihardt's ashes, along with those of his wife, Mona, were scattered into the swirling currents.[20] Today, his daughter Hilda lives along its banks.

Early in *The River and I* Neihardt writes, "I have come to look upon the Missouri as more than a river. To me, it is an epic." So, too, is it now for all of us.

NOTES

1. *Neihardt: A Journey Home*, Nebraska ETV Network, KUON-TV, Lincoln, Nebraska, 1970, videocassette.

2. *Neihardt: A Journey Home.*

3. Frank Waters, "Neihardt and the Vision of Black Elk," in *A Sender of Words: Essays in Memory of John G. Neihardt* (Salt Lake City: Howe Brothers, 1984), 14.

4. John G. Neihardt, *Patterns and Coincidences* (Columbia: University of Missouri Press, 1978), 53.

5. Caspar Whitney to John G. Neihardt, 23 March 1908, John G. Neihardt Papers, Western Historical Manuscript Collection, University of Missouri–Columbia.

6. John G. Neihardt, "The Epic-Minded Scot," in *The Ancient Memory and Other Stories* (Lincoln: University of Nebraska Press, 1991), 135.

7. Frank Luther Mott, *A History of American Magazines, vol. 5, 1905–1930* (Cambridge: Harvard University Press, Belknap Press, 1968), 637–38.

8. [Jeanette Gilder], "The Lounger," *Putnam's and The Reader* 4, no. 4 (July 1908): 506.

9. Edgeley W. Todd, "The Frontier Epic: Frank Norris and John G. Neihardt," *Western Humanities Review* 13 (winter 1959): 43.

10. John G. Neihardt to Horst Franz, 6 August 1939, John G. Neihardt Papers, Western Historical Manuscript Collection, University of Missouri–Columbia.

11. John G. Neihardt, *All Is But a Beginning* (New York: Harcourt Brace Jovanovich, 1972), 26.

12. Blair Whitney, *John G. Neihardt* (Boston: Twayne Publishers, 1976), 84.

13. Julius T. House, *John G. Neihardt: Man and Poet* (Wayne NE: F. H. Jones and Son, 1920), 80.

14. House, *John G. Neihardt*, 7.

15. Review of *The River and I*, *The Dial* 49, no. 588 (16 December 1910): 525.

16. Richard Burton, "The Bellman's Bookshelf," review of *The River and I*, *The Bellman* 10, no. 255 (3 June 1911): 690.

17. "Notes," review of *The River and I*, *The Nation* (8 December 1910): 556.

18. [Jeanette Gilder], "The Lounger," *Putnam's Magazine* (December 1909): 382.

19. House, *John G. Neihardt*, 7.

20. Hilda Neihardt, *Black Elk and Flaming Rainbow: Personal Memories of the Lakota Holy Man and John Neihardt* (Lincoln: University of Nebraska Press, 1995), 116.

CONTENTS

ILLUSTRATIONS

Illustrations xix

THE RIVER AND I

CHAPTER I

THE RIVER OF AN UNWRITTEN EPIC

IT was Carlyle—was it not?—who said that all great works produce an unpleasant impression, on first acquaintance. It is so with the Missouri River. Carlyle was not, I think, speaking of rivers; but he was speaking of masterpieces—and so am I.

It makes little difference to me whether or not an epic goes at a hexameter gallop through the ages, or whether it chooses to be a flood of muddy water, ripping out a channel from the mountains to the sea. It is merely a matter of how the great dynamic force shall express itself.

I have seen trout streams that I thought

were better lyrics than I or any of my fellows can ever hope to create. I have heard the moaning of rain winds among mountain pines that struck me as being equal, at least, to *Adonais*. I have seen the solemn rearing of a mountain peak into the pale dawn that gave me a deep religious appreciation of my significance in the Grand Scheme, as though I had heard and understood a parable from the holy lips of an Avatar. And the vast plains of my native country are as a mystic scroll unrolled, scrawled with a cabalistic writ of infinite things.

In the same sense, I have come to look upon the Missouri as more than a river. To me, it is an epic. And it gave me my first big boy dreams. It was my ocean. I remember well the first time I looked upon my turbulent friend, who has since become as a brother to me. It was from a bluff at Kansas City. I know I must have been a very little boy, for the terror I felt made me reach up to the saving forefinger of my father, lest this insane devil-thing before me should suddenly develop an unreasoning hunger for little boys.

My father seemed as tall as Alexander—and quite as courageous. He seemed to fear it almost not at all. And I should have felt little surprise had he taken me in his arms and stepped easily over that mile or so of liquid madness. He talked calmly about it— quite calmly. He explained at what angle one should hold one's body in the current, and how one should conduct one's legs and arms in the whirlpools, providing one should swim across.

Swim across! Why, it took a giant even to talk that way! For the summer had smitten the distant mountains, and the June floods ran. Far across the yellow swirl that spread out into the wooded bottom-lands, we watched the demolition of a little town. The siege had reached the proper stage for a sally, and the attacking forces were howling over the walls. The sacking was in progress. Shacks, stores, outhouses, suddenly developed a frantic desire to go to St. Louis. It was a weird retreat in very bad order. A cottage with a garret window that glared like the eye of a Cyclops, trembled, rocked with the athletic lift of the

flood, made a panicky plunge into a convenient tree; groaned, dodged, and took off
through the brush like a scared cottontail.
I felt a boy's pity and sympathy for those
houses that got up and took to their legs across
the yellow waste. It did not seem fair. I
have since experienced the same feeling for a
jack-rabbit with the hounds a-yelp at its heels.

But—to *swim* this thing! To fight this
cruel, invulnerable, resistless giant that went
roaring down the world with a huge uprooted
oak tree in its mouth for a toothpick! This
yellow, sinuous beast with hell-broth slaver-
ing from its jaws! This dare-devil boy-god
that sauntered along with a town in its pocket,
and a steepled church under its arm for a
moment's toy! Swim *this?*

For days I marvelled at the magnificence of
being a fullgrown man, unafraid of big rivers.

But the first sight of the Missouri River was
not enough for me. There was a dreadful
fascination about it—the fascination of all
huge and irresistible things. I had caught
my first wee glimpse into the infinite; I was
six years old.

" OFF ON THE PERILOUS FLOODS "

5

Many a lazy Sunday stroll took us back to the river; and little by little the dread became less, and the wonder grew—and a little love crept in. In my boy heart I condoned its treachery and its giant sins. For, after all, it sinned through excess of strength, not through weakness. And that is the eternal way of virile things. We watched the steamboats loading for what seemed to me far distant ports. (How the world shrinks!) A double stream of "roosters" coming and going at a dog-trot rushed the freight aboard; and at the foot of the gang-plank the mate swore masterfully while the perspiration dripped from the point of his nose.

And then—the raucous whistles blew. They reminded me of the lions roaring at the circus. The gang-plank went up, the hawsers went in. The snub nose of the steamer swung out with a quiet majesty. Now she feels the urge of the flood, and yields herself to it, already dwindled to half her size. The pilot turns his wheel—he looks very big and quiet and masterful up there. The boat veers round; bells jangle. And now the engine wakens in earnest. She breathes with spurts of vapor !

Breathed? No, it was sighing; for about it all clung an inexplicable sadness for me—the sadness that clings about all strong and beautiful things that must leave their moorings and go very, very far away. (I have since heard it said that river boats are not beautiful!) My throat felt as though it had smoke in it. I felt that this queenly thing really wanted to stay; for far down the muddy swirl where she dwindled, dwindled, I heard her sobbing hoarsely.

Off on the perilous flood for "faërie lands forlorn"! It made the world seem almost empty and very lonesome

And then the dog-days came, and I saw my river tawny, sinewy, gaunt — a half-starved lion. The long dry bars were like the protruding ribs of the beast when the prey is scarce, and the ropy main current was like the lean, terrible muscles of its back.

In the spring it had roared; now it only purred. But all the while I felt in it a dreadful economy of force, just as I have since felt

"BARRIERS FORMED BEFORE HIM"

it in the presence of a great lean jungle-cat
at the zoo.   Here was a thing that crouched
and purred—a mewing but terrific thing.
Give it an obstacle to overcome—fling it
something to devour; and lo! the crushing
impact of its leap!

And then again I saw it lying very quietly
in the clutch of a bitter winter—an awful
hush upon it, and the white cerement of the
snow flung across its face.   And yet, this
did not seem like death; for still one felt in it
the subtle influence of a tremendous personality.   It slept, but sleeping it was still a
giant.   It seemed that at any moment the
sleeper might turn over, toss the white cover
aside and, yawning, saunter down the valley with its thunderous seven-league boots.
And still, back and forth across this heavy
sleeper went the pigmy wagons of the farmers
taking corn to market!

But one day in March the far-flung arrows
of the geese went over. *Honk! honk!* A
vague, prophetic sense crept into the world
out of nowhere—part sound, part scent, and
yet too vague for either.   Sap seeped from the

maples. Weird mist-things went moaning
through the night. And then, for the first
time, I saw my big brother win a fight!

For days, strange premonitory noises had
run across the shivering surface of the ice.
Through the foggy nights, a muffled intermittent booming went on under the wild
scurrying stars. Now and then a staccato
crackling ran up the icy reaches of the river,
like the sequent bickering of Krags down a
firing line. Long seams opened in the dis-
turbed surface, and from them came a
harsh sibilance as of a line of cavalry unsheath-
ing sabres.

But all the while, no show of violence—
only the awful quietness with deluge potential in it. The lion was crouching for
the leap.

Then one day under the warm sun a booming as of distant big guns began. Faster and
louder came the dull shaking thunders, and
passed swiftly up and down, drawling into
the distance. Fissures yawned, and the
sound of the grumbling black water beneath
came up. Here and there the surface lifted

BOATS WRECKED IN AN ICE GORGE

13

—bent—broke with shriekings, groanings, thunderings. And then——

The giant turned over, yawned and got to his feet, flinging his arms about him! Barriers formed before him. Confidently he set his massive shoulders against them—smashed them into little blocks, and went on singing, shouting, toward the sea. It was a glorious victory. It made me very proud of my big brother. And yet all the while I dreaded him—just as I dread the caged tiger that I long to caress because he is so strong and so beautiful.

Since then I have changed somewhat, though I am hardly as tall, and certainly not so courageous as Alexander. But I have felt the sinews of the old yellow giant tighten about my naked body. I have been bent upon his hip. I have presumed to throw against his Titan strength the craft of man. I have often swum in what seemed liquid madness to my boyhood. And we have become acquainted through battle. No friends like fair foes reconciled!

And I have lain panting on his bars, while

all about me went the lisping laughter of my brother. For he has the strength of a god, the headlong temper of a comet; but along with these he has the glad, mad, irresponsible spirit of a boy. Thus ever are the epic things.

The Missouri is unique among rivers. I think God wished to teach the beauty of a virile soul fighting its way toward peace— and His precept was the Missouri. To me, the Amazon is a basking alligator; the Tiber is a dream of dead glory; the Rhine is a fantastic fairy-tale; the Nile a mummy, periodically resurrected; the Mississippi, a convenient geographical boundary line; the Hudson, an epicurean philosopher.

But the Missouri—my brother—is the eternal Fighting Man!

I love all things that yearn toward far seas: the singing Tennysonian brooks that flow by "Philip's farm" but "go on forever"; the little Ik Walton rivers, where one may "study to be quiet and go a-fishing"! the Babylonian streams by which we have all pined in captivity; the sentimental Danubes

AFTER THE SPRING BREAK-UP

which we can never forget because of "that night in June"; and at a very early age I had already developed a decent respect for the verbose manner in which the "waters come down at Lodore."

But the Missouri is more than a sentiment— even more than an epic. It is the symbol of my own soul, which is, I surmise, not unlike other souls. In it I see flung before me all the stern world-old struggle become materialized. Here is the concrete representation of the earnest desire, the momentarily frustrate purpose, the beating at the bars, the breathless fighting of the half-whipped but never-to-be-conquered spirit, the sobbing of the wind-broken runner, the anger, the madness, the laughter. And in it all the unwearying urge of a purpose, the unswerving belief in the peace of a far away ocean.

If in a moment of despair I should reel for a breathing space away from the fight, with no heart for battle-cries, and with only a desire to pray, I could do it in no better manner than to lift my arms above the river and cry out into the big spaces: "You who somehow understand—behold this river! It expresses what is voiceless in me. It prays for me!"

Not only in its physical aspect does the Missouri appeal to the imagination. From Three Forks to its mouth—a distance of three thousand miles—this zigzag watercourse is haunted with great memories. Perhaps never before in the history of the world has a river been the thoroughfare of a movement so tremendously epic in its human appeal, so vastly significant in its relation to the development of man. And in the building of the continent Nature fashioned well the scenery for the great human story that was to be enacted here in the fulness of years. She built her stage on a large scale, taking no account of miles; for the coming actors were to be big men, mighty travellers, intrepid fighters, laughers at time and space. Plains limited only by the rim of sky; mountains severe, huge, tragic as fate; deserts for the trying of strong spirits; grotesque volcanic lands — dead, utterly ultra-human — where athletic souls might struggle with despair;

impetuous streams with their rapids terrible
as Scylla, where men might go down fighting:
thus Nature built the stage and set the scenes.
And that the arrangements might be complete,
she left a vast tract unfinished, where still
the building of the world goes on—a place
of awe in which to feel the mighty Doer of
Things at work. Indeed, a setting vast and
weird enough for the coming epic. And as the
essence of all story is struggle, tribes of wild
fighting men grew up in the land to oppose
the coming masters; and over the limitless
wastes swept the blizzards.

I remember when I first read the words
of Vergil beginning *Ubi tot Simois*, "where
the Simois rolls along so many shields and
helmets and strong bodies of brave men
snatched beneath its floods." The far-seeing sadness of the lines thrilled me; for it
was not of the little stream of the *Æneid*
that I thought while the Latin professor
quizzed me as to constructions, but of that
great river of my own epic country — the
Missouri. Was I unfair to old Vergil, think
you? As for me, I think I flattered him a

bit! And in this modern application, the ancient lines ring true. For the Missouri from Great Falls to its mouth is one long grave of men and boats. And such men!

It is a time-honored habit to look back through the ages for the epic things. Modern affairs seem a bit commonplace to some of us. A horde of semi-savages tears down a town in order to avenge the theft of a faithless wife who was probably no better than she should have been—and we have the *Iliad*. A petty king sets sail for his native land, somehow losing himself ten years among the isles of Greece—and we have the *Odyssey*. (I would back a Missouri River "rat" to make the same distance in a row boat within a month!) An Argive captain returns home after an absence of ten years to find his wife interested overmuch in a trusted friend who went not forth to battle; a wrangle ensues; the tender spouse finishes her lord with an axe—and you have the *Agamemnon*. (To-day we should merely have a sensational trial, and hysterical scareheads in the newspapers.) Such were the ancient stories that move us all—sordid enough, be sure, when you push them hard for facts.   But time and genius have glorified them.   Not the deeds, but Homer and Æschylus were great.

We no longer write epics—we live them. To create an epic, it has been said somewhere, the poet must write with the belief that the immortal gods are looking over his shoulder.

We no longer prostrate ourselves before the immortal gods.   We have long since discovered the divinity within ourselves, and so we have flung across the continents and the seas the visible epics of will.

The history of the American fur trade alone makes the Trojan War look like a Punch and Judy show! and the Missouri River was the path of the conquerors.   We have the facts—but we have not Homer.

An epic story in its essence is the story of heroic men battling, aided or frustrated by the superhuman.   And in the fur trade era there was no dearth of battling men, and the elements left no lack of superhuman obstacles.

I am more thrilled by the history of the

Lewis and Clark expedition than by the tale
of Jason. John Colter, wandering three
years in the wilderness and discovering the
Yellowstone Park, is infinitely more heroic
to me than Theseus. Alexander Harvey
makes Æneas look like a degenerate. It was
Harvey, you know, who fell out with the
powers at Fort Union, with the result that
he was ordered to report at the American Fur
Company's office at St. Louis before he could
be reinstated in the service. This was at
Christmas time—Christmas of a Western
winter. The distance was seventeen hundred miles, as the crow flies. "Give me a
dog to carry my blankets," said he, "and
by God I'll report before the ice goes out!"
He started afoot through the hostile tribes
and blizzards. He reported at St. Louis
early in March, returning to Union by the
first boat out that year. And when he arrived at the Fort, he called out the man who
was responsible for the trouble, and quietly
killed him. That is the stern human stuff
with which you build realms. What could
not Homer do with such a man? And when

one follows him through his recorded career,
even Achilles seems a bit ladylike beside him!

The killing of Carpenter by his treacherous
friend, Mike Fink, would easily make a whole
book of hexameters—with a nice assortment
of gods and goddesses thrown in. There
was a woman in the case—a half-breed.
Well, this half-breed woman fascinates me
quite as much as she whose face "launched a
thousand ships and burnt the topless towers
of Ilium"! In ancient times the immortal
gods scourged nations for impieties; and, as we
read, we feel the black shadow of inexorable
fate moving through the terrific gloom of
things. But the smallpox scourge that broke
out at Fort Union in 1837, sweeping with
desolation through the prairie tribes, moves
me more than the storied catastrophes of old.
It was a Reign of Terror. Even Larpenteur's bald account of it fills me with the
fine old Greek sense of fate. Men sickened
at dawn and were dead at sunset. Every
day a cartload or two of corpses went over
the bluff into the river; and men became
reckless. Larpenteur and his friend joked daily

about the carting of the gruesome freight. They felt the irresistible, and they laughed at it, since struggle was out of the question. Some drank deeply and indulged in hysterical orgies. Some hollowed out their own graves and waited patiently beside them for the hidden hand to strike. At least fifteen thousand died — Audubon says one hundred and fifty thousand; and the buffalo increased rapidly — because the hunters were few.

Would not such a story — here briefly sketched—move old Sophocles?

The story of the half-breed woman—a giantess—who had a dozen sons, has about it for me all the glamour of an ancient yarn. The sons were free-trappers, you know, and, incidentally, thieves and murderers. (I suspect some of our classic heroes were as much!) But they were doubtless living up to the light that was in them, and they were game to the finish. So was the old woman; they called her "the mother of the devils." Trappers from the various posts organized to hunt them down, and the mother and the sons

barricaded their home. The fight was a
hard one. One by one the "devils" fell
fighting about their mother. And then the
besieging party fired the house. With all
her sons wounded or dead, the old woman
sallied forth. She fought like a grizzly and
went down like a heroine.

A sordid, brutal story? Ah, but it was life!
Fling about this story of savage mother-love
the glamour of time and genius, and it will
move you, believe me!

And the story of old Hugh Glass! Is it
not fateful enough to be the foundation of a
tremendous Æschylean drama? A big man
he was—old and bearded. A devil to fight,
a giant to endure, and an angel to forgive!
He was in the Leavenworth campaign against
the Aricaras, and afterward he went as a
hunter with the Henry expedition. He had a
friend—a mere boy—and these two were very
close. One day Glass, who was in advance
of the party, beating up the country for game,
fell in with a grizzly; and when the main party
came up, he lay horribly mangled with the
bear standing over him. They killed the bear,

but the old man seemed done for; his face had all the features scraped off, and one of his legs went wobbly when they lifted him.

It was merely a matter of one more man being dead, so the expedition pushed on, leaving the young friend with several others to see the old man under ground. But the old man was a fighter and refused to die, though he was unconscious: scrapped stubbornly for several days, but it seemed plain enough that he would have to let go soon. So the young friend and the others left the old man in the wilderness to finish up the job by himself. They took his weapons and hastened after the main party, for the country was hostile.

But one day old Glass woke up and got one of his eyes open. And when he saw how things stood, he swore to God he would live, merely for the sake of killing his false friend. He crawled to a spring near by, where he found a bush of ripe bull-berries. He waited day after day for strength, and finally started out to *crawl* a small matter of one hundred miles to the nearest fort. And he did it, too!

Also he found his friend after much wandering —and forgave him.

Fancy Æschylus working up that story with the Furies for a chorus and Nemesis appearing at intervals to nerve the old hero!

And Rose the Renegade, who became the chief of a powerful tribe of Indians! And Father de Smet, one of the noblest figures in history, carrying the gospel into the wilderness! And Le Barge, the famous pilot, whose biography reads like a romance! In the history of the Missouri River there were hundreds of these heroes, these builders of the epic West. Some of them were violent at times; some were good men and some were bad. But they were masterful always. They met obstacles and overcame them. They struck their foes in front. They thirsted in deserts, hungered in the wilderness, froze in the blizzards, died with the plagues, and were massacred by the savages. Yet they conquered. Heroes of an unwritten epic! And their pathway to defeat and victory was the Missouri River.

If you wish to have your epic spiced with

the glamour of kings, the history of the river
will not fail you; for in those days there
were kings as well as giants in the land.
Though it was not called such, all the blank
space on the map of the Missouri River
country and even to the Pacific, was one
vast empire — the empire of the American
Fur Company; and J. J. Astor in New York
spoke the words that filled the wilderness
with deeds. Thus democratic America once
beheld within her own confines the paradox
of an empire truly Roman in character.

Here and there on the banks of the great
waterway—an imperial road that would have
delighted Cæsar—many forts were built.
These were the ganglia of that tremendous
organism of which Astor was the brain. The
bourgeois of one of these posts was virtually
proconsul with absolute power in his terri-
tory. Mackenzie at Union—which might
be called the capital of the Upper Missouri
country —was called "King of the Missouri."
He had an eye for seeing purple. At one
time he ordered a complete suit of armor
from England; and even went so far as to have

medals struck, in true imperial fashion, to be distributed among his loyal followers.

Far and wide these Western American kings flung the trappers, their subjects, into the wilderness. Verily, in the unwritten "Missouriad" there is no lack of regal glamour.

The ancients had a way of making vast things small enough to be familiar. They made gods of the elements, and natural phenomena became to them the awful acts of the gods.

These moderns made no gods of the elements—they merely conquered them! The ancients idealized the material. These moderns materialized the ideal. The latter method is much more appealing to me—an American — than the former. I love the ancient stories; but it is for the modern marvellous facts that I reserve my admiration.

When one looks upon his own country as from a height of years, old tales lose something of their wonder for him. It is owing to this attitude that the prospect of descending the great river in a power canoe from the head of navigation gave me delight.

Days and nights filled with the singing and muttering of my big brother! And I would need only to close my eyes, and all about me would come and go the ghosts of the mighty doers— who are my kin. Big men, bearded and powerful, pushing up stream with the cordelle on their shoulders! Voyageurs chanting at the paddles! Mackinaws descending with precious freights of furs! Steamboats grunting and snoring up stream! Old forts sprung up again out of the dusk of things forgotten, with all the old turbulent life, where in reality to-day the plough of the farmer goes or the steers browse! Forgotten battles blowing by in the wind! And from a bluff's summit, here and there, ghostly war parties peering down upon me—the lesser kin of their old enemies— taking a summer's outing where of old went forth the fighting men, the builders of the unwritten epic!

CHAPTER II

SIXTEEN MILES OF AWE

OUR party of three left the railroad at Great Falls, a good two-days' walk up river from Benton, the head of Missouri River navigation, to which point our boat material had been shipped and our baggage checked.

A vast sun-burned waste of buffalo-grass, prickly pears, and sagebrush stretched before us to the north and east; and on the west the filmy blue contour of the Highwoods Mountains lifted like sun-smitten thunder clouds in the July swelter. One squinting far look, however, told you that these were not rain clouds. The very thought of rain came to you with the vagueness of some birth-surviving memory of a former time. You looked far up and out to the westward and caught the glint of snow on the higher peaks. But the sight was unconvincing; it was like a story told without the "vital impulse." Always had these plains blistered under this July sun; always had the spots of alkali made the only whiteness; and the dry harsh snarl and snap of the grasshoppers' wings had pricked this torrid silence through all eternity.

A stern and pitiless prospect for the amateur pedestrian, to be sure; for we devotees of the staff and pack have come to associate pedestrianism with the idyllic, and the idyllic flourishes only in a land of frequent showers. Theocritus and prickly pears are not compatible. Yet it was not without a certain thrill of exaltation that we strapped on our packs and stretched our legs after four days on the dusty plush.

And though ahead of us lay no shady, amiably crooked country roads and bosky dells, wherein one might lounge and dawdle over Hazlitt, yet we knew how crisscross cattle-trails should take us skirting down the river's sixteen miles of awe.

Five hundred miles below its source, the falls of the Missouri begin with a vertical plunge of sixty feet. This is the Black Eagle Falls, presumably named so by Lewis and Clark and other explorers, because of the black eagles found there.

With all due courtesy to my big surly grumbling friend, the Black Eagle Falls, I must say that I was a bit disappointed in him. Oh! he is quite magnificent enough, and every inch a Titan, to be sure; but of late years it seems he has taken up with company rather beneath him. First of all, he has gone to work in a most plebeian, almost slave-like fashion, turning wheels and making lights and dragging silly little trolley cars about a straggling town. Also, he hobnobs continually with a sprawling, brawling, bad-breathed smelter, as no respectable Titan should do. And on top of it all—and this was the straw that broke the back of my sentimental camel—he allows them to maintain a park on the cliffs above him, where the merest white-skinned, counter-jumping pigmy may come of a Sunday for his glass of pop and a careless squint at the toiling Titan. Puny Philistines eating peanuts and watching

Samson at his Gaza stunt! I like it not. Rather would I see the Muse Clio pealing potatoes or Persephone busy with a banana cart! Enceladus wriggling under a mountain is well enough; but Enceladus composedly turning a crank for little men—he seemed too heavy for that light work.

Leaning on the frame observation platform, I closed my eyes, and in the dull roar that seemed the voices of countless ages, the park and the smelter and the silly bustling trolley cars and the ginger-ale and the peanuts and my physical self—all but my own soul— were swallowed up. I saw my Titan brother as he was made—four hundred yards of writhing, liquid sinew, strenuously idle, mag- nificently worthless, flinging meaningless thunders over the vast arid plain, splendidly empty under sun and stars! I saw him as La Verendrye must have seen him—busy only at the divine business of being a giant. And for a moment behind shut eyes, it seemed very inconsequential to me that cranks should be turned and that trolley cars should run up and down precisely in the same place,

BLACK EAGLE FALLS

37

never getting anywhere, and that there should be anything in all that tract but an austere black eagle or two, and my own soul, and my Titan brother.

When I looked again, I could half imagine the old turbulent fellow winking slily at me and saying in that undertone you hear when you forget the thunders for a moment: "Don't you worry about me, little man. It's all a joke, and I don't mind. Only to-morrow and then another to-morrow, and there won't be any smelters or trolley cars or ginger-ale or pea-nuts or sentimentalizing outers like yourself. But I'll be here howling under sun and stars."

Whereupon I posed the toiling philosopher before the camera, pressed the bulb, and des-scended from the summit of the cliff (as well as from my point of view) to the trail skirting northward up the river, leaving Enceladus grumbling at his crank.

Perhaps, after all, cranks really have to be turned. Still, it seems too bad, and I have long bewailed it almost as a personal grief, that utility and ugliness should so often be running mates.

They tell me that the Matterhorn never did a tap of work; and you could n't color one Easter egg with all the gorgeous sunsets of the world! May we all become, some day, perfectly useless and beautiful!

At the foot of the first fall, a mammoth spring wells up out of the rock. Nobody tells you about it; you run across it by chance, and it interests you much more in that way. It would seem that a spring throwing out a stream equivalent to a river one hundred yards wide and two feet deep would deserve a little exploitation. Down East they would have a great white sprawling hotel built close by it wherein one could drink spring water (at a quarter the quart), with half a pathology pasted on the bottle as a label. But nobody seems to care much about so small an ooze out there: everything else is so big. And so it has nothing at all to do but go right on being one of the very biggest springs of all the world. This is really something; and I like it better than the quarter-per-quart idea.

In sixteen miles the Missouri River falls four hundred feet. Incidentally, this stretch of river is said to be capable of producing the most tremendous water-power in the world.

After skirting four miles of water that ran like a mill-race, we came upon the Rainbow Falls, where a thousand feet of river takes a drop of fifty feet over a precipice regular as a wall of masonry. This was much more to my liking—a million horse-power or so busy making rainbows! Bully!

It was a very hot day and the sun was now high. I sat down to wipe the sweat out of my eyes. (One does not *perspire* in July up there; one *sweats!*) I wished to get acquainted with this weaver of iridescent nothings who knew so well the divine art of doing nothing at all and doing it good and hard! After all, it isn't so easy to do nothing and make it count!

And in the end, when all broken lights have blended again with the Source Light, I'm not so sure that rainbows will seem less important than rows and rows of arc lights and clusters and clusters of incandescent globes. Are you? I can contract an indefinable sort of heartache from the blue sputter of a city light that snuffs out moon and stars for tired scurrying folks: but the opalescent mist-drift of the Rainbow Falls wove heavens for me in its sheen, and through its whirlwind rifts and crystal flaws, far reaches opened up with all the heart's desire at the other end. You shut your eyes with that thunder in your ears and that gusty mist on your face, and you see it very plainly—more plainly than ever so many arc lights could make you see it—the ultimate meaning of things. To be sure, when you open your eyes again, it's all gone—the storm-flung rainbows seem to hide it again.

A mile below, we came upon the Crooked Falls of twenty feet. Leaving the left bank, and running almost parallel with it for some three hundred yards, then turning and making a horseshoe, and returning to the right bank almost opposite the place of first observation, this fall is nearly a mile in length, being an unbroken sheet for that distance. This one, also, does nothing at all, and in a beautifully irregular way. Somehow it made me think of Walt Whitman! But we left it soon, swinging out into the open parched country. We knew all this turbulence to be merely the river's bow before the great stunt.

As we swung along, kicking up the acrid alkali dust from the cattle-trail that snaked its way through the cactus and sagebrush, the roar behind us died; and before us, far away, dull muffled thunders grew up in the hush of the burning noon. Thunders in a desert, and no cloud! For an hour we swung along the trail, and ever the thunders increased—like the undertone of the surf when the sea whitens. We were approaching the Great Falls of the Missouri. There were no sign posts in that lonesome tract; no one of whom to ask the way. Little did we need direction. The voice of thunder crying in the desert led us surely.

A half-hour more of clambering over shale-strewn gullies, up sun-baked watercourses, and we found ourselves toiling up the ragged slope of a bluff; and soon we stood upon a rocky ledge with the thunders beneath us. Damp gusts beat upward over the blistering scarp of the cliff. I lay down, and crawling to the edge, looked over. Two hundred feet below me—straight down as a pebble drops—a watery Inferno raged, and far-flung whirlwinds, all but exhausted with the dizzy upward reach, whisked cool, invisible mops of mist across my face.

Flung down a preliminary mile of steep descent, choked in between soaring walls of rock four hundred yards apart, innumerable crystal tons rushed down ninety feet in one magnificent plunge. You saw the long bent crest—shimmering with the changing colors of a peacock's back—smooth as a lake when all winds sleep; and then the mighty river was snuffed out in gulfs of angry gray. Capricious river draughts, sucking up the damp defile, whipped upward into the blistering sunlight gray spiral towers that leaped into opal fires and dissolved in showers of diamond and pearl and amethyst.

I caught myself tightly gripping the ledge and shrinking with a shuddering instinctive fear. Then suddenly the thunders seemed to stifle all memory of sound—and left only

GREAT FALLS FROM CLIFF ABOVE

45

the silent universe with myself and this terribly beautiful thing in the midst of utter emptiness. And I loved it with a strange, desperate, tigerish love. It expressed itself so magnificently; and that is really all a man, or a waterfall, or a mountain, or a flower, or a grasshopper, or a meadow lark, or an ocean, or a thunderstorm has to do in this world. And it was doing it right out in the middle of a desert, bleak, sun-leprosied, forbidding, with only the stars and the moon and the sun and a cliff-swallow or two to behold. Thundering out its message into the waste places, careless of audiences—like a Master! Bully, grizzled old Master-Bard singing—as most of them do—to empty benches! And it had been doing that ten thousand thousand years, and would do so for ten thousand thousand more, and never pause for plaudits. I suspect the soul of old Homer did that—and is still doing it, somehow, somewhere. After all there is n't much difference between really tremendous things—Homer or waterfalls or thunderstorms—is there? It's only a matter of how things happen to be big.

I was absent-mindedly chasing some big thundering line of Sophocles when Bill, the little Cornishman, ran in between me and the evasive line: "Lord! what a waste of power!"

There is some difference in temperaments. Most men, I fancy, would have enjoyed a talk with a civil engineer upon that ledge. I should have liked to have Shelley there, myself. It's the difference between poetry and horse-power, dithyrambics and dynamos, Keats and Kipling! What is the energy exerted by the Great Falls of the Missouri? How many horse-power did Shelley fling into the creation of his *West Wind?* How many foot-pounds did the boy heart of Chatterton beat before it broke? Please leave something to the imagination!

We backtrailed to a point where the cliff fell away into a rock-strewn incline, and clambered down a break-neck slope to the edge of the crystal broil. There was a strange exhilaration about it—a novel sense of discovering a natural wonder for ourselves. We seemed the first men who had ever been

GREAT FALLS FROM THE FRONT

there: that was the most gripping thing about it.

Aloof, stupendous, terrific, staggering in the intensity of its wild beauty, you reach it by a trail. There are no 'busses running and you can't buy a sandwich or a peanut or a glass of beer within ten miles of its far-flung thunders. For twentieth century America, that is doing rather well!

Skirting the slippery rocks at the lip of the mad flood, we swung ourselves about a ledge, dripping with the cool mist-drift; descended to the level of the lower basin, where a soaking fog made us shiver; pushed through a dripping, oozing, autumnal sort of twilight, and came out again into the beat of the desert sun, to look squarely into the face of the giant.

A hawk wheeled and swooped and floated far up in the dazzling air. Somehow that hawk seemed to make the lonely place doubly lonely. Did you ever notice how a lone coyote on a snow-heaped prairie gives you a heartache, whereas the empty waste would only have exhilarated you? Always, it seemed, that

veering hawk had hung there, and would
hang so always—outliving the rising of suns
and the drifting of stars and the visits of the
moon.

A vague sense of grief came over me at the
thought of all this eternal restlessness, this
turbulent fixity; and, after all, it seemed much
greater to be even a very little man, living
largely, dying, somehow, into something big
and new; than to be this Promethean sort of
thing, a giant waterfall in a waste.

I have known men who felt dwarfed in the
presence of vast and awful things. I never
felt bigger than when I first looked upon the
ocean. The skyward lift of a mountain peak
makes me feel very, very tall. And when a
thunderstorm comes down upon the world
out of the northwest, with jagged blades of
fire ripping up the black bellies of the clouds,
I know all about the heart of Attila and the
Vikings and tigers and Alexander the Great!
So I think I grew a bit, out there talking
to that water-giant who does nothing at all—
not even a vaudeville stunt — and does it so
masterfully.

By and by they'll build a hotel in the flat at the edge of the lower basin; plant prim flowers in very prim beds; and rob you on the genteel European plan. Comfortably sitting in a willow chair on the broad veranda, one will read the signs on those cliffs—all about the best shoes to wear, and what particular pill of all the pills that be, should be taken for that ailing kidney. But it will not be I who shall sit in that willow chair on that broad, as yet unbuilt, veranda.

The sun was glinting at the rim of the cliffs, and the place of awe and thunders was slowly filling with shadow. We found a steep trail, inaccessible for vehicles, leading upward in the direction of Benton. It was getting that time of day when even a sentimentalist wants a beefsteak, especially if he has hiked over dusty scorching trails and scrambled over rocks all day.

Some kind man back in the town, with a fund of that most useless article, information, had told us of a place called Goodale, theoretically existing on the Great Northern Railroad between Great Falls and Benton. We had provided only for luncheon, trusting to fate and Goodale for supper.

Goodale! A truly beautiful name! No doubt in some miraculous way the character of the country changed suddenly just before you got there merely to justify the name. Surely no one would have the temerity to conjure up so beautiful a name for a desert town. Yet, half unwillingly, I thought of a little place I once visited — against my will, since the brakeman put me off there—by the name of Forest City. I remembered with misgivings how there wasn't a tree within something like four hundred miles. But I pushed that memory aside as a lying prophet. I believed in Goodale and beefsteak. Goodale would be a neat, quiet little town, set snugly in a verdant valley. We would come into it by starlight—down a careless gypsying sort of country road; and there would be the sound of a dear little trickling bickering cool stream out in the shadows of the trees fringing the approach to Goodale. And we'd pass pretty little cottages with vines growing over the doors, and hollyhocks peeping over the fences, and cheerful lights in the windows.

Goodale! And then, right in the middle of the town (no, *village*—the word is cosier somehow)—right in the middle of the village there would be a big restaurant, with such alluring scents of beefsteak all about it.

I set the pace up that trail. It was a swinging, loose, cavalry-horse sort of pace— the kind that rubs the blue off the distance and paints the back trail gray. Goodale was a sort of Mecca. I thought of it with something like a religious awe. How far was Goodale, would you suppose? Not far, certainly, once we found the railroad.

We made the last steep climb breathlessly, and came out on the level. A great, monotonous, heartachy prairie lay before us — utterly featureless in the twilight. Far off across the scabby land a thin black line swept out of the dusk into the dusk — straight as a crow's flight. It was the railroad. We made a cross-cut for it, tumbling over gopher holes, plunging through sagebrush, scrambling over gullies that told the incredible tale of torrents having been there once.   I ate quantities of alkali dust and went on believing in Goodale and beef-steak.   Beefsteak became one of the princi-pal stations on the Great Northern Railroad, so far as I was concerned personally.   That is what you might call the geography of a healthy stomach.

With the falling of the sun the climate of the country had changed. It was no longer blistering. You sat down for a moment and a shiver went up your spine.   At noon I thought about all the lime-kilns I had ever met. Now I could hear the hickory nuts dropping in the crisp silence down in the old Missouri woods.

We struck the railroad and went faster. Since my first experience with railroad ties, I have continued to associate them with hunger. I need only look an ordinary railroad tie in the face to contract a wonderful appetite. It works on the principle of a memory system.   So, as we put the ties behind us, I increased my order at that restaurant in the sweet little pedestrian's village of

Goodale. "A couple of eggs on the side, waiter," I said half audibly to the petite woman in the white apron who served the tables in the restaurant there. She was very real to me. I could count the rings on her fingers; and when she smiled, I noted that her teeth were very white—doubtless they got that way from eating quantities and quantities of thick juicy beefsteak!

The track took a sudden turn ahead. "Around that bend," said I aloud, "lies Goodale." We went faster. We rounded the bend, only to see the dusky, heartachy, barren stretch.

"Railroads," explained I to myself, "have a way of going somewhere; it is one of their peculiarities." No doubt this track had been laid for the express purpose of guiding hungry folks to the hospitable little village. We plunged on for an hour. Meanwhile my orders to the trim little woman in the white apron increased steadily. She smiled broadly but winsomely, showing those charming beefsteak-polished teeth. They shone like a beacon ahead of me, for it was now dark.

Suddenly we came upon a signboard.　We went up to it, struck a match, and read breathlessly—"GOODALE."

We looked about us.　Goodale was a switch and a box car.

Nothing beside remains,

I quoted audibly:

'round the decay
Of that colossal wreck, boundless and bare,
The lone and level sands stretch far away.

Alas for the trim little lady with the white teeth and the smile and the beefsteak!

We said bitter things there in that waste about the man with the information.　We loaded his memory with anathemas.　One cannot eat a signboard, even with so inviting a name upon it.　An idea struck me—it seemed a very brilliant one at the moment. I sat down and delivered myself of it to my companions, who also had lusted after the flesh-pots.　"We have wronged that man with the information," said I.　"He was no ordinary individual; he was a prophet: he simply got his dates mixed.　In precisely one hundred years from now, there will be a town on this spot—and a restaurant! Shall we wait?"

They cursed me bitterly.   I suspect neither of them is a philosopher.   Thereat I proceeded to eat a thick juicy steak from the T-bone portion of an unborn steer, served by the trim little lady of a hundred years hence, there in that potential village of Goodale. And as I smoked my cigarette, I felt very thankful for all the beautiful things that do not exist.

And I slept that night in the great front bedroom, the ceiling of which is of diamond and turquoise.

CHAPTER III

HALF-WAY TO THE MOON

A^T last the sinuous yellow road dropped over the bluff rim and, to all appearances, dissolved into the sky—a gray-blue, genius-colored sky.

It was sundown, and this was the end of the trail for us. Beneath the bluff rim lay Benton. We flung ourselves down in the bunch-grass that whispered drily in a cool wind fresh from the creeping night-shade. Now that Benton lay beneath us, I was in no hurry to look upon it.

Fort Benton? What a clarion cry that name had been to me! Old men—too old for voyages—had talked about this place; a long time ago, 'way down on the Kansas City docks, I had heard them. How far away it was then! Reach after reach, bend after bend, grunting, snoring, toiling, sparring over bars, bucking the currents, dodging the snags, went the snub-nosed steamers—brave little steamers!—forging on toward Fort Benton. And it was so very, very far away—half-way to the moon no doubt! St. Louis was indeed very far away. But Fort Benton!——

Well, they spoke of the Fort Benton traffic as "the mountain trade," and I had not then seen a mountain. You could stand on the very tallest building in Kansas City, and you could look and look and never see a mountain. And to think how far the brave little steamers had to go! How *did* they ever manage to get back?

But the old men on the docks—they had been there and all the way back, perhaps hundreds of times. And they were such heroes! Great paw-like hands they had, toughened with the gripping of cables; eyes that had that way of looking through and far beyond things. (Seamen and plainsmen have it.) And they had such romantic, crinkly, wrinkly, leathery faces. They got so on the way to Benton and back. And they talked about it—those old men lounging on the docks—because it was so far away and they were so old that they could n't get there any more.

What a picture I made out of their kaleidoscopic chatter; beautifully inaccurate, impossibly romantic picture, in which big muscley men had fights with yawping painted savages that always got gloriously licked, in the approved story-book manner! I could shut my eyes and see it all very plainly, away off there half-way to the moon. And I used to wonder how my father could be such a strong man and never have any hankering to go up there at all! The two facts were quite incompatible. He should have been a captain and taken me on for cub pilot, or at least a "striker" engineer; though I would n't have objected seriously to the business of a cabin boy. I thought it would be very nice to engage in the mountain trade.

And then, after a while, in the new light that creeps in with years, I began to rearrange my picture of things up there; and Benton crept a wee bit closer—until I could see its

OLD FORT BENTON IN THE 70'S

four adobe walls and its two adobe bastions, stern with portholes, sitting like bulldogs at the opposite corners ready to bark at intruders. And in and out at the big gate went the trappers—sturdy, rough-necked, hirsute fellows in buckskins, with Northwest fusils on their shoulders; lean-bodied, capable fellows, with souls as lean as their bodies, survivors of long hard trails, men who could go far and eat little and never give up. I was very fond of that sort of man.

Little by little the picture grew. Indian bull boats flocked at the river front beneath the stern adobe walls; moored mackinaws swayed in the current, waiting to be loaded with peltries and loosed for the long drift back to the States; and keel-boats, looking very fat and lazy, unloaded supplies in the late fall that were loaded at St. Louis in the early spring. And these had come all the way without the stroke of a piston or the crunch of a paddle-wheel or a pound of steam. Nothing but grit and man-muscle to drag them a small matter of two or three thousand miles up the current of the most eccentric old duffer of a river in the world!

5

What men it did take to do that! I saw them on the wild shelterless banks of the yellow flood—a score or so of them—stripped and sweating under the prairie sun, with the cordelle on their calloused shoulders, straightening out to the work like honest oxen. What *males* those cordelle men were —what *stayers!* Fed on wild, red meat, lean and round of waist, thick of chest, thewed for going on to the finish! Ten or fifteen miles a day and every inch a fight! Be sure they did n't do it merely for the two or three hundred dollars a year they got from the Company. They did it because they were that sort of men, and had to express themselves. Everything worth while is done that way.

Do they raise that breed now? Never doubt it! You need only find your keel-boats or their equivalents, and the men will come around for the job, I 'm sure. But when you speak enthusiastically of the old Greek doers of things, I 'd like to put in a few words for those old up-river men. They belong to the unwritten American epic.

And then the keel-boats and the bull-boats

and the mackinaws and the up-river men flashed out—like a stereopticon picture when the man moves the slide; and I saw a little ragged village of log houses scattered along the water front. I saw the levees piled with merchandise, and a score or more of packets rushing fresh cargoes ashore—mates bawling commands down the gangplanks where the roustabouts came and went at a trot. Gold-mad hundreds thronged the wagon-rutted streets of this raw little village, the commercial centre of a vast new empire. Six-horse freighters trundled away toward the gold fields; and others trundled in, their horses jaded with the precious freight they pulled. And I saw steamers dropping out for the long voyage back to the States, freighted with cargoes of gold dust—really truly story-book treasure-ships that would have made old Captain Kidd's men mad with delight.

As I lay dreaming in the bunch-grass, it all grew up so real that I had to get up and take my first look, half expecting to find it all there just as in the old days.

We stood at the rim of the bluff and looked

down into a cup-like valley upon a quiet little village, winking with scattered lights in the gloaming. Past it swept the river— glazed with the twilight and silver-splotted with early stars.

This was Benton—it could have been almost any other town as well. And yet, once upon a time, it had filled my day-dreams with wonders—this place that seemed half-way to the moon.

The shrill shriek of a Great Northern locomotive, trundling freight cars through the gloom, gave the death-stroke to the old boy-dream. It was the cry of modernity. This boisterous, bustling, smoke-breathing thing, plunging through the night with flame in its throat, had made the change, dragged old Benton out of the far-off lunar regions and set what is left of it right down in the back yard of the world. Even a very little boy could get there now.

"And yet," thought I, as we set out rapidly for the village in the valley, "the difference between the poetry of mackinaws and Great Northern locomotives is merely a matter of

"THIS WAS BENTON"

perspective.   If those old cordelle men could only come back for a while from their Walhalla, how they would crowd about that wind-splitting, fire-eating, iron beast, panting from its long run, and catching its breath for another plunge into the waste places and the night! And I? I would be gazing wide-mouthed at the cordelle men. It's only the human curiosity about the other side of the moon.   How perfect the nights would be if we could only see that lost Pleiad!"

Ankle-deep in the powdery sand, we entered the little town with its business row facing the water front.   One glance at the empty levees told you of the town's dead glory.   Not a steamboat's stacks, blackening in the gloom, broke the peaceful glitter of the river under the stars.   But along the sidewalk where the electric-lighted bar-rooms buzzed and hummed, brawny cow-men, booted and spurred, lounged about, talking in that odd but not unpleasant Western English that could almost be called a dialect.

But it was not the Benton of the cow-men that I felt about me.   It was still for me the

Benton of the fur trade and the steamboats and the gold rush—my boyhood's Benton half-way to the moon—the ghost of a dead town.

At Goodale I had sought a substantial town and found a visionary one. At Benton I had sought a visionary town and found a substantial one. Philosophy was plainly indicated as the proper thing. And, after all, a steaming plate of lamb chops in a Chinese chuck-house of a substantial though disappointing town, is more acceptable to even a dreamer than the visionary beefsteak I ate out there in that latent restaurant of a potential village.

This was a comfortable thought; and for a quarter of an hour, the far weird cry of things that are no more, was of no avail. The rapid music of knife and fork drowned out the asthmatic snoring of the ghostly packets that buck the stream no more. How grub does win against sentiment!

Swallowing the last of the chops, "Where will I find the ruins of the old fort?" I asked of my bronze-faced neighbor across the wreck of supper. He looked bored and

RUINS OF FORT BENTON

stiffened a horny practical thumb in the general direction of the ruins. "Over there," he said laconically.

I caught myself wondering if a modern Athenian would thus carelessly direct you to the Acropolis. Is the comparison faulty? Surely a ruin is sacred only for what men did there. We are indeed a headlong race. We keep our ruins behind us. Perhaps that is why we get somewhere. And yet, what beauty blooms flowerlike to the backward gaze! Music and poetry—all the deepest, purest sentiments of the heart—are fed greatly upon the memory of the things that were but can never be again. Mnemosyne is the mother of all the Muses.

I got up and went out. By the light of a thin moon, I found the place "over there." An odd, pathetic little ruins it is, to be sure. Nothing imposing about it. It does n't compel through admiration: it wooes through pity—the great, impersonal kind of pity.

> "A single little turret that remains
> On the plains"—

Browning tells about all there is to tell

about it, though he never heard of it; only they called it a "bastion" in old days—the little square adobe blockhouse that won't stand much longer. One crumbling bastion and two gaunt fragments of adobe walls in a waste of sand beside the river—that's Fort Benton.

A thin pale grudging strip of moon lit it up: just the moon by which to see ruins—a moon for backward looking and regrets. A full round love-moon would n't have served at all.

Out of pure moon-haze I restored the walls of the house where the bourgeois lived. The fireplace and the great mud chimney are still there, and the smut of the old log fires still clings inside. The man who sat before that hearth was an American king. A simple word of command spoken in that room was the thunder of the law in the wilderness about and men obeyed. There's a bat living there now. He tumbled about me in the dull light, filling the silence with the harsh whir of pinions.

I thought about that night a long, long time ago when all the people under the protection of the newly erected fort, gathered

THE HOUSE OF THE BOURGEOIS

77

here for a house-warming. How clearly I could hear that squawking, squeaking, good-natured fiddle and the din of dancing feet! Only the sound got mixed up with the dim, weird moonlight, until you did n't know whether you were hearing or seeing or feeling it—the music of the fiddles and the feet. Oh, the dim far music!

I thought about the other ruins of the world, the exploited, tourist-haunted ruins; and I wondered why the others attract so much attention while this one attracts practically none at all. How they do dig after old Troy—poor old long-buried, much-abused Troy! And nobody even cares to steal a brick from this ruined citadel that took so great a part in the American epic. Indeed, you would not be obliged to steal a brick; there are no guards.

Some one has said that the history of our country as taught in the common schools is the history of a narrow strip of land along the Atlantic coast. The statement is significant. The average school-teacher knows very little about Fort Benton, I suspect.

And yet, one of the most tremendous of all human movements centred about it—the movement that brought about the settlement of the Northwest. One of these days they will plant a potato patch there!

But modern Benton?

Get on a train in the East, snuggle up in your berth, plunge on to the Western coast, and you run through the real West in the night. They are getting Eastern out there at the rim of the big sea. Benton is in the West—the big, free, heart-winning West; and it gives promise of staying there for a while yet.

Charter a bronco and canter out across the river for an hour, and it will be very plain to you that the romantic West still lives— the West of the cowboy and the bronco and the steer. Not the average story-book West, to be sure. Perhaps that West never existed. But it is the West that has bred and is still breeding a race of men as beautiful in a virile way (and how else should men be beautiful?) as this dear old mother of an Earth ever suckled.

A ROUND-UP OUTFIT ON THE MARCH

I stood once on the yellow slope of a hill and watched a round-up outfit passing in the gulch below.   Four-horse freighters grumbling up the dusty trail; cook wagons trundling after; whips popping over the sweating teams; a hundred or more saddle ponies trailing after in rolling clouds of glinting dust; a score of bronze-faced, hard-fisted outriders, mounted on gaunt, tough, wise little horses— such strong, outdoor, masterful Americans, truly beautiful in a big manly way!

The sight of it all put that glorious little achy feeling in my throat that you get when they start the fife and drum, or when a cavalry column wheels at the word of command, or when a regiment swings past with even tread, or when you stand on a dock and watch a liner dropping out into the fog.   It's the feeling that you're a man and mighty proud of it.   But somehow it always makes you just a little sad.

I felt proud of that bunch of strong capable fellows—proud as though I had created them myself.

And once again the glorious little achy

feeling in the throat came.   The Congressman from Choteau County had returned from Washington with fresh laurels; and Benton turned out to welcome her Great Man. Down the dusty, poorly lighted, front street came the little band—a shirt-sleeved squad. Halting under the dingy glow of a corner street-lamp, they struck up the best-intentioned, noisiest noise I ever heard.   The tuba raced lumberingly after the galloping cornet, that ran neck-and-neck with the wheezing clarinet; and the drums beat up behind, pounding like the hoofs of stiff-kneed horses half a stretch behind.

It was a mad, exciting race of sounds— a sort of handicap.   The circular glow of the street-lamp became the social centre of Benton. At last the mad race was ended.   I think it was the cornet that won, with the clarinet a close second.   The tuba, as I recollect it, complacently claimed third money, and the bass-drum finished last with a shameless, resolute boom!

A great hoarse cry went up—probably for the winning cornet; a big-lunged, generous,

warrior cry that made you think of a cavalry
charge in the face of bayonets. And the
shirt-sleeved band swung off down the
street in the direction of the little cottage
where the Great Man lived. All Benton
fell in behind—clerks and bar-keeps and sheepmen and cowboys tumbling into fours. Under
the yellow flare of the kerosene torches they
went down the street like a campaigning company in rout step, scattering din and dust.

Great, deep-chested, happy-looking, open
air fellows, they were; big lovers, big haters,
good laughers, eaters, drinkers—and every
one of them potentially a fighting man.

And suddenly, as I watched them pass,
something deep down in me cried out:
"Great God! What a fighting force we can
drum up out of the cactus and the sagebrush
when the time comes!" And when I looked
again, not one of the sun-bronzed faces was
strange to me, but every one was the face of
a brother. Choteau's Congressman was my
Congressman! Benton's Great Man was my
Great Man! I fell into line alongside a big
bronco-buster with his high - heeled boots

and his clanking spurs and his bandy-legged, firm-footed horseman's stride.   Thirty yards farther on we were old comrades.   That is the Western way.

Once again the little band struck up a march, which was very little more than a rhythmic snarling and booming of the drums, with now and then the shrill savage cry of the clarinet stabbing the general din.   Irresistibly the whole line swung into step.

What is it about the rhythmic stride of many men down a dusty road that grips you by the throat and makes your lungs feel like overcharged balloons?   I felt something like the maddening, irritating tang of powder-smoke in my throat.   Trumpet cries that I had never heard, yet somehow dimly remembered, wakened in the night about us—far and faint, but haughty with command.   It took very little imagination for me to feel the whirlwind of battles I may never know, to hear the harsh metallic snarl of high-power bullets I may never face.   For, marching there in the dusty, torch-painted night, with that ragged procession of Westerners, a deep sense of the essential comradeship of free men had come upon me; and I could think of these men in no other way than as potential fighting men—the stern hard stuff with which you build and keep your empires. What a row little old Napóleon could have kicked up with half a million of these sage-brush boys to fling foeward under his cannon-clouds!

We reached the cottage of the Great Man with the fresh laurels. He met us at the gate. He called us Jim and Bill and Frank and Kid something or other. We called him Charlie. And he was n't the least bit stiff or proud, though we had n't the least doubt that half of Washington was in tears at his departure for the West.

The sudden flare of a torch betrayed his moist eyes as he told us how he loved us. And I 'm sure he meant it. He said, with that Western drawl of his: "Boys, while I was back there trying to do a little something for you in Congress, I heard a lot of swell bands; but I did n't hear any such music as this little old band of ours has made to-night!" The

unintentional humor somehow did n't make
you want to laugh at all.

We're all riding with his outfit; and next
year we're going to send Charlie back East
again.   May we all die sheepmen if we don't
—and that's the limit in Montana!

Talking about sheepmen, reminds me of
Joe, the big bronco-buster, and his *mot*.   I
was doing the town with Joe, and he was
carefully educating me in the Western mys-
teries.   He told me all about "day-wranglers"
and "night-hawks" and "war-bags" and
"round-ups"; showed me how to tie a "bull-
noose" and a "sheep-shank" and a "Mexican
hacamore"; put me onto the twist-of-the-
wrist and the quick arm-thrust that puts
half-hitches 'round a steer's legs; showed
me how a cowboy makes dance music with a
broom and a mouth-harp—and many other
wonderful feats, none of which I can myself
perform.

I wanted to feel the mettle of the big typical
fellow, and so I said playfully: "Say, Joe, come
to confession—you're a sheepman, now
are n't you?"

JOE

He clanked down a glass of long-range liquid, and glared down at me with a monitory forefinger pointing straight between my eyes: "Now you look here, Shorty," he drawled; "you're a friend of mine, and whatever you say, *goes*, as long as I ain't all caved in! But you cut that out, and don't you say that out loud again, or you and me'll be having to scrap the whole outfit!"

He resumed his glass. I told him, still playfully, that a lot of mighty good poetry had been written about sheep and sheepmen and crooks and lambs and things like that, and that I considered my question complimentary.

"You're talkin' about sheepmen in the old country, Shorty," he drawled. "There ain't any cattle ranges there, you know. Do you know the difference between a sheepman in Scotland, say, and in Montana?"

I did not.

"Well," he proceeded, "over in Scotland when a feller sees a sheepman coming down the road with his sheep, he says: 'Behold the gentle shepherd with his fleecy flock!'

That's poetry. Now in Montana, that same feller says, when he sees the same feller coming over a ridge with the same sheep: '*Look at that crazy blankety-blank with his woolies!*' That's fact. You mind what I say, or you'll get spurred."

I don't quite agree with Joe, however. Once, lying in my tent across the river, I looked out over the breaks through that strange purple moonlight, such as I had always believed to exist only in the staging of a melodrama, and saw four thousand sheep descending to the ferry.

Like lava from a crater they poured over the slope above me; and above them, seeming prodigiously big against the weird sky, went the sheepman with his staff in his hand and a war-bag over his arm, while at his heels a wise collie followed. It was a picture done by chance very much as Millet could have done it. And somehow Joe's *mot* couldn't stand before that picture.

There is indeed a big Pindaric sort of poetry about a plunging mass of cattle. And just as truly there is a sort of Theocritus poetry

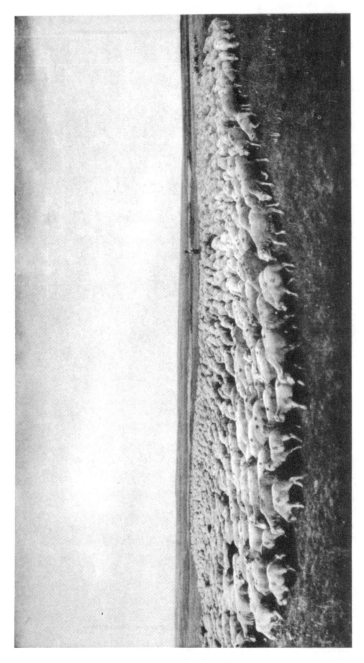

MONTANA SHEEP

about sheep. Only in the latter case, the poetical vanishing point is farther away for me than is the case with cattle. I think I couldn't write very good verses about a flock of sheep, unless I were at least five hundred yards from them. I haven't figured the exact distance as yet. But when you have a large flock of sheep camping about you all night, making you eat fine sand and driving you mad with that most idiotic of all noises (which happened once to me), you don't get up in the morning quoting Theocritus. You remember Joe's *mot!*

We found a convenient gravel bar on the farther side of the river, where we established our navy-yard. There we proceeded to set up the keel of the *Atom I*—a twenty-foot canoe with forty-inch beam, lightly ribbed with oak and planked with quarter-inch cypress.

No sooner had we screwed up the bolts in the keel, than our ship-yard became a sort of free information bureau. Every evening the cable ferry brought over a contingent of

well-wishers, who were ardent in their desire
to encourage us in our undertaking, which
was no less than that of making a toboggan
slide down the roof of the continent.

The salient weakness of the *genus homo*,
it has always seemed to me, is an overwhelming desire to give advice. Through several
weeks of toil, we were treated to a most liberal education on marine matters. It appeared that we had been laboring under a
fatal misunderstanding regarding the general
subject of navigation. Our style of boat
was indeed admirable — for a lake, if you
please, *but*—well, of course, they did not wish
to discourage us. It was quite possible that
we were unacquainted with the Upper Missouri. Now the Upper River (hanging out
the bleached rag of a sympathetic smile),
the Upper River was *not* the Lower River,
you know. (That really *did* seem remarkably
true, and we became alarmed.) The Upper
River, mind you, was terrific. Why, those
frail ribs and that impossible planking would
go to pieces on the first rock—like an egg-
shell! Of course, we were free to do as we

MONTANA WOOL-FREIGHTER

pleased—they would not discourage us for
the world.   And   the   engine!   Gracious!
Such a boat would never stand the vibration
of a four-horse, high-speed engine driving a
fourteen-inch screw!   It appeared plainly that
we were almost criminally wrong in all our
calculations.   Shamefacedly we continued to
drive nails into the impossible hull, knowing
full well—poor misguided heroes—that we
were only fashioning a death trap!   There
could be no doubt about it.   The free information bureau was unanimous.   It was all very
pathetic.   Nothing but the tonic of an habit-
ual morning swim in the clear cold river kept
us game in the face of the inevitable!

We saw it all.   With a sort of forlorn,
cannon-torn-cavalry-column hope we pushed
on with the fatal work.   Never before did I
appreciate old Job in the clutches of good
advice.   I used to accuse him of rabbit
blood.   In the light of experience, I wish to
record the fact that I beg his pardon.   He
was in the house of his friends.   I think
Job and I understand each other better now.
It was not the boils, but the free advice!

At last the final nail was driven and clenched, the canvas glued on and ironed, the engine installed. The trim, slim little craft with her admirable speed lines, tapering fore and aft like a fish, lay on the ways ready for the plunge.

We had arranged to christen her with beer. The Kid stood at the prow with the bottle poised, awaiting his cue. The little Cornishman knelt at the prow. He was *not* bowed in prayer. He was holding a bucket under the soon-to-be-broken bottle. "For," said he, "in a country where beer is so dear and advice so cheap, let us save the beer that we may be strong to stand the advice!"

The argument was indeed Socratic.

"And now, little boat," said I, in that dark brown tone of voice of which I am particularly proud, "be a good girl! Deliver me not unto the laughter of my good advisers. I christen thee *Atom!*"

The bottle broke—directly above that bucket.

And now before us lay the impossible as plainly pointed out, not only by local talent,

THE "ATOM I" UNDER CONSTRUCTION

but by no less a man than the august captain
of a government snag-boat. Several weeks
before the launching, an event had taken
place at Benton. The first steamboat for
sixteen years tied up there one evening. She
was a government snag-boat. Now a government snag-boat may be defined as a boat
maintained by the government for the sole
purpose of navigating rivers *and dodging snags*.
This particular snag-boat, I learned afterward in the course of a long cruise behind her,
holds the snag-boat record. I consider her
pilot a truly remarkable man. He seemed
to have dodged them all.

All Benton turned out to view the big
red and white government steamer. There
was something almost pathetic about the
public demonstration when you thought
of the good old steamboat days. During
her one day's visit to the town, I met the
captain.

He was very stiff and proud. He awed
me. I stood before him fumbling my hat.
Said I to myself: "The personage before me
is more than a snag-boat captain. This is

none other than the gentleman who invented the Missouri River. No doubt even now he carries the patent in his pocket!"

"Going down river in a power canoe, eh?" he growled, regarding me critically. "Well, you 'll never get down!"

"That so?" croaked I, endeavoring to swallow my Adam's apple.

"No, you won't!"

"Why?" ventured I timidly, almost pleadingly; "Is n't there—uh—is n't there—uh—*water enough?*"

"Water enough—yes!" growled the personage who invented the longest river in the world and therefore knew what he was talking about. "Plenty of water—*but you won't find it!*"

Now as the *Atom* slid into the stream, I thought of the captain's words. Since that time the river had fallen three feet. We drew eighteen inches.

Sixty-five days after that oraculous utterance of the captain, the Kid and I, half stripped, sunburned, sweating at the oars, were forging slowly against a head wind at the mouth of the Cheyenne, sixteen hundred miles below the head of navigation. A big white and red steamer was creeping up stream over the shallow crossing of the Cheyenne's bar, sounding every foot of the water fallen far below the usual summer level.

It was the snag-boat. Crossing her bows and drifting past her slowly, I stood up and shouted to the party in the pilot house:

"I want to speak to the captain."

He came out on the hurricane deck—the man who invented the river. He was still stiff and proud, but a swift smile crossed his face as he looked down upon us, half-naked and sun-blackened there in our dinky little craft.

"Captain," I cried, and perhaps there was the least vain-glory in me; "I talked to you at Benton."

"Yes sir."

"Well, *I have found that water!*"

CHAPTER IV

MAKING A GETAWAY

TELL a Teuton that he can't, and very likely he will show you that he can. It's in the blood. Between the prophecy of the snag-boat captain and my vain-glorious answer at the Cheyenne crossing, I learned to respect the words of the man who invented the eccentric old river. In the face of heavy head winds, I quoted the words, "You'll never get down"—and they bit deep like whip lashes. On many a sand-bar and gravel reef, with the channel far away, I heard the words, "Plenty of water, yes, but you won't find it!" And always something stronger than my muscles cried out within me: "The devil I won't, O you inventor of rain-water creeks!" Hour by hour, day by day, against almost continual head winds and with the lowest water in years, that discouraging prophecy invaded my ego and was repulsed. And that is why we have pessimists in the world. A pessimist is merely a counter-irritant.

I stood on the bank for some time after the *Atom I* slid into the water, admiring her truly beautiful lines. Once I was captain of a trunk lid that sailed a frog-pond down in Kansas City; and at that time I thought I knew the meaning of pride. I did not. All three of us were a bit puffed up over that boat. Something of that pride that goes before a fall awoke in my captain's breast as I loved her with my eyes—that trim, slim speed-thing, tugging at her forward line, graceful and slender and strong and fleet as a Diana.

I said at last: "I will now get in her, drop down to the town landing, and proceed to put to shame a few of these local motor-tubs that make so much fuss and don't get anywhere!"

I loved her as a man should love all things that are swift and strong and honest, keen for marks and goals—a big, clean-limbed, thor-

oughbred horse that will break his heart to
get under the wire first; a high-power rifle,
slim of muzzle, thick of breech, with its
wicked little throaty cry, doing its business
over a flat trajectory a thousand yards away:
I loved her as a man should love those.
Little did I dream that she would betray me.

I took in the line and went aboard. At
that moment I almost understood the snag-
boat captain's bearing. To be master of the
Atom I seemed quite enough; but to be the
really truly captain of a big red and white
snag-boat—it must have been overwhelming!

I dropped out into the current that, fresh
from its plunge of four hundred feet in sixteen
miles, ran briskly. Everything was in readi-
ness. I meant to put a crimp in the vanity of
that free-information bureau.

I turned on the switch, opened the needle
valve, swung the throttle over to the notch
numbered with a big "2." I placed the crank
on the wheel and gave it a vigorous turn.

"Poof!" said the engine sweetly, and the
kind word encouraged me immensely. Again
I cranked.

"Poof! Poof!"

It seemed that I had somehow misunderstood the former communication, and it was therefore repeated with emphasis. Like a model father who walks the floor with the weeping child, tenderly seeking the offending pin, I looked over that engine. "What have I neglected?" said I. I intended to be quite logical and fair in the matter.

I once presided over a country newspaper that ran its presses with a gasoline engine with a most decided artistic temperament. That engine used to have a way of communing silently with its own soul right in the middle of press day. I remembered this with forebodings. I remembered how firm but kind I was obliged to be with that old engine. I remembered how it always put its hands in its pockets and took an extended vacation every time I swore at it. I decided to be nothing but a perfect gentleman with this engine. I even endeavored to be a jovial good fellow.

"What is it, Little One?" said I mentally; "does its little carburetor hurt it? Or did the bad man strangle it with that horrid old gasoline?"

I tenderly jiggled its air valve, fiddled gently with its spark-control lever. I cranked it again. It barked at me like a dog! I had been kind to it, and it barked right in my face. I wanted to slap it. I lifted my eyes and saw that the rapid current would soon carry me past the town landing. I seized a paddle and shoved her in. Of course, a member of the free-information bureau was at the landing. He had with him a bland smile and a choice bit of information.

"Having trouble with your engine, are n't you?" he said as I leaped ashore with the line. "There must be something wrong with it!" The remark was indeed illuminating. It struck me with the force of an inspiration. It seemed so true.

"Strange that I had n't thought of that!" I remarked. "That really must be the trouble—there 's something wrong with it. Thanks!"

I tied the boat and went up-town, hoping to sidetrack the benevolent member of that

ubiquitous bureau. When I returned, I
found half a dozen other benevolent members
at the landing. They were holding a consultation, evidently; and the very air felt
gummy with latent advice.

"What's the matter with your engine?"
they chorused.

"Why, there's something wrong with it!"
I explained cheerfully, as I went aboard
again. I began to crank, praying steadily
for a miracle. Now and then I managed to
coax forth a gaseous chortle or two. The
convention on the landing understood every
chortle in a truly marvellous way.

"It's the spark-plug, that's sure!" announced one with an air of finality. "When
an engine has run for a while (!) the spark-
plug gets all smutted up. Have you cleaned
your spark-plug?"

"No Jim!" contradicted another, "it's
all in the oil feed! Look how she puffs!
W'y it's in the oil feed—plain as day! Now
if you'll take off that carburetor and——"

I cranked on heroically.

"It's in the timer," volunteered another.

"You see that little brass lever back there? Well, you take and remove that and you 'll find that——"

I cranked on shamelessly.

"The batteries ain't no good!" growled a man with a big voice that reminded me of a bass-drum booming up among the wind instruments in a medley. Like the barber who owned the white owl, I stuck to my business. I cranked on.

"It ain't *in* them batteries—them batteries is all right!" piped a weazened little man who had been grinning wisely at the lack of mechanical ability so shamelessly exposed by his fellows. "Now in a jump-spark engine," he explained leisurely, with a knowing squint of his eyes and an uplifted explanatory forefinger: "in a jump-spark engine, gentlemen, there is a number of things to consider. Now if you 'll take and remove that cylinder-head, pull out the piston, and——"

The voice of the expounder was suddenly drowned out by the earsplitting rapid-fire of the exhaust! The miracle had happened! Hooray!

I grasped the steering cords and jammed her rudder hard to port. Her fourteen-inch screw, suddenly started at full speed ahead, made the light, slim craft leap like a spike-spurred horse.

But the turn was too short. She thrust her sharp haughty nose into the air like an offended lady, and started up the bank after that information bureau. If a tree had been convenient, I think she would have climbed it.

I shut her down.

"*She went that time!*" chorused the information bureau. Coming from an information bureau, the statement was marvellously correct. But I had suddenly become too glad-hearted for a sharp retort.

"If you will please throw me the line, and push me off," I said confidently, "I 'll drop out into the current."

I dropped out.

"Now for putting a crimp in some people's vanity!" I exulted.

I cranked. Nothing doing! I cranked some more. No news from the crimping department. I continued to crank; also, I

8

continued to drift. Somehow that current seemed to have increased alarmingly in speed.

I thought I heard a sound of merriment. I looked up. The little weazened man was gesticulating wildly with that forefinger of his. He was explaining something. The information bureau, steadily dwindling into the distance, was not listening. It seemed to be enjoying itself immensely.

I swallowed a half-spoken word that tasted bitter as it went down. Then I cranked again. There seemed to be nothing else to do. It was a hot day; hot sweat blinded me, and trickled off the tip of my nose. My hands began to develop blisters. Finally, a deep disgust seized me. I once saw a tender-hearted lady on her knees in the dust before a balky auto. I remembered her half-sobbed words: "*You mean thing, you! What is the matter with you, anyway! Oh, you mean, mean thing!*"

I sat down in front of that engine and abandoned myself to a great feeling of tenderness and chivalry for that unfortunate lady. In that moment I believe I would have fought a bear for her! Oh that all the gasoline engines in the world could be concentrated somehow into one big woolly, scary black bear, how I could have set my teeth in its neck and died chewing!

I heard a roaring of waters that broke my vision of bear fights and gentle ladies in distress. A hundred yards ahead of me I saw rapids. The words of the information bureau came back to me with terrible distinctness: "Why, her light timbers will go to pieces on the first rock!"

Although I am no hero, I did n't get frightened. I got sore. "Go ahead, and smash yourself up, if you like!" I cried to the balky craft. And then I waited to see her do it. She swung 'round sharply with the first suck of the rapids, struck a rock, side-stepped, struck another, and went on down, grinding and dragging on a stony reef.

It suddenly came to me that this was what they called the Grocondunez Rapids. I remembered that they said the name meant "the big bridge of the nose." The name had a powerful fascination for me—I wanted to hit something good and hard somewhere in that region!

Finally she swung clear of the reef, caught the swirl of the main current, and started for New Orleans with the bit in her teeth. I was n't ready to arrive in New Orleans at once; I had made other arrangements. So I grasped a paddle and drove her into shallow water. I leaped out, waist-deep in the cold stream, and threw my weight against her. Pantingly, I wondered what was the exact distance to the nearest axe. I resolved to crank her once more and then for the axe hunt!

I leaned over the gunwale and began to grind. For the life of me, I don't know just what I did to her; but it seemed that she had taken some offence. Without the least warning, she leaped forward at three-quarter speed, and started up stream with that haughty head of hers thrust skyward!

I clung desperately to her gunwale, and she dragged me insultingly in the drink! She made a soppy rag of me! I managed to scramble aboard—something after the fashion of a bronco-buster who mounts at a gallop.

But the way she *travelled!* I forgot the ducking and forgave her with all my heart. I held her nose well out into the channel where the current ran with swells, though no wind blew.

Bucking the rapids, she split the fast water over her nose and sent it aft in two clean-cut masses, that hissed about her like angry skirts. A light, V-shaped wake spread after, scarcely agitating the surface. She dragged no water. There was no churning at her stern. Only the dull, subaqueous drone, felt rather than heard beneath the rapid banging of her exhaust, told me how the honest little screw thrust hard.

I pushed the spark-lever close to the reversing point, and opened her throttle wide. This acted like a bottle-fly on the flank of a spirited mare. She shook herself, quivering through all her light, pliable construction, lifted her prow another inch or two, and flung the rapids behind her.

Slim, fleet, clean-heeled, and hungry for distance, she raced toward the Benton landing two miles up.

In my anxiety to show her to the benevolent ones, I left the current and took a crosscut over a rocky ford. Pebbles flung from her pounding heels showered down upon me. I climbed forward and let her hammer away. She cleared the gravel bar, and as she plunged past the now silent information bureau on the landing, condescendingly I waved a hand at them and went on splitting water.

We shot under the bridge, forged into the crossing current, passed the big brick hotel, where a considerable number came out to salute us. They dubbed her the fastest boat that had ever climbed that current, I learned afterward. Alas! I was getting my triumph early and in one big chunk! I figure that that one huge breakfast of triumph, if properly distributed, would have fed me through the whole two thousand miles of back-strain and muscle-cramp. And yet, through all the days of snail-paced toil that followed, I remained truly thankful for that early breakfast.

The Kid and the Cornishman, busy in camp with the packing for the voyage, had shared in the gloom of my temporary defeat. But now, as I plunged past them, I could see them leaping into the air and cracking their heels together with delight. They had wet every plank of her with their sweat, and they were as proud as I. In the light of the following days, their delight dwindled into a pathetic thing.

I held her on her course up-stream, reached the bend a mile above, swung round and—discovered that she had only then begun to lift her heels! With the rapid current to aid, her speed was truly wonderful. She could have kept pace with any respectable freight train at least.

I indulged in a little feverish mental calculation. She could make, with the minimum current, eighteen miles per hour. Every day meant fifteen hours of light. Sioux City was two thousand miles away. We could reach Sioux City easily in ten days of actual running!

While I was covering that fast mile back to camp, I saw the *Atom I* passing Sioux City with an air of high-nosed contempt.

I developed a sort of unreasoning hunger
for New Orleans—a kind of violent thirst
for the Gulf of Mexico! Nothing short of
these, it seemed to me, could be worthy of so
fleet a craft. When I shoved her nose into
the landing, I found that my companions
thoroughly agreed with me.

All that night in my restless sleep I drove
speed boats at a terrific pace through impossible channels and rock-toothed Scyllas;
and the little Cornishman fought angry seas
and heard a dream-wind shrieking in the
cordage, and felt the salt spume on his face.
"I wonder why I am always dreaming that,"
he said. "Atavism," I ventured; and he
regarded me narrowly, as though I might
be maligning his character in some way.

At dawn we had already eaten and were
loading the *Atom* for the voyage. With her
cargo she drew eighteen inches of water. At
full speed, she would squat four inches. It was
the first of August and the water, which had
reached in the spring its highest point for
twenty years, had been falling rapidly, and
now promised to go far below the average

THE CABLE FERRY TOWED US OUT

low-water mark.   We had ahead of us a long
voyage, every mile of which was strange
water.

Once again I went over that feverish calculation.   This time I was more generous.
I decided upon fifteen days.   The cable
ferry towed us out beyond the gravel bars
that, during the last week, had been slowly
lifting their bleached masses higher.   In
mid-stream we cut loose.

At the first turn the engine started.   We
were going at a good half-speed clip, when
suddenly the engine changed its mind.
"Squash!" it said wearily.   Then it let off a
gasoline sigh and went into a peaceful sleep.
We had reached the brick hotel.   We pulled
in with the paddles and tied up.   The information bureau was there, and at once
went into consultation.

"I'm looking for an engine doctor," I said.
"How about Mr. Blank?   They tell me he
knows the unknowable."

"Best man with an engine in town," said
one.

"For gracious' sake, keep that man away

from your engine if you don't want it ruined!" said others. A man who can arouse a diversity of opinions is at least a man of originality. I went after that man.

He came—with an air of mystery and a monkey wrench. He sat down in front of the patient (how that word *does* fit!) and after some time he said: "*Hm!*"

He unscrewed this—and whistled awhile; he unscrewed that—and whistled some more. Then he screwed up both this and that and cranked her.

"Phew-oo-oo-oo!" said the engine. Whereat the doctor smiled knowingly. It was plain that she was an open book to him.

"What is the trouble?" said I, with that tone of voice you use in a sick-room.

It appeared to be appendicitis.

"Spark-plug," muttered the doctor.

"Shall I get another?" I asked, half apologetically.

"Better," grunted the doctor.

I chased down an automobile owner, and a launch owner and a man who had a small pumping-engine. I was eloquent in my appeal for spark-plugs. I made a very fine collection of them[1] and hastened back to the doctor. He did n't seem to appreciate my efforts. He had the patient on the operating-table. Everything was either unscrewed or pulled out. He was carefully scrutinizing the wreck—for more things to screw out!

"Locate the trouble?" I ventured.

"Buzzer 's out of whack," replied the Man of Awe; "Have to get another spark-coil!" In times of sickness even the sternest man submits to medical tyranny. I ran down a man who once owned a power boat, and he had a spark-coil. He finally agreed to forego the pleasure of possessing it for a suitable reward. Considering the size of that reward, he had undoubtedly become greatly attached to his spark-coil!

I returned in triumph to the doctor. He was now screwing up all that he had previously unscrewed.

"Think she 'll go now?" I pleaded.

[1] Dear Reader: Should you undertake the Missouri River trip, don't lay anything out on spark-plugs. I sowed them all along up there. Take a drag-net. You will scoop up several hundred dry batteries, but don't mind them; they are probably spoiled.

He screwed up several dozen things, and whistled a while. Then the oracle gave voice: "'Fraid the batteries won't do; they 're awful weak!"

With a bitter heart, I turned on my heel and went forth once more. Electrical supplies were not on sale at any of the stores. But I found a number of gentlemen who were evidently connoisseurs in the battery business. They had batteries of which they were extremely fond. They parted with some of superior quality upon the consideration of a friendly regard for me—and a slight emolument on my part. I was evidently very popular.

At a breathless speed I returned to—*not* to the doctor. He had vanished. Rumor had it that he had gone home to lunch, for the sun was now high. So far as I know, he is still at lunch.

Several things were yet unscrewed. I fell to work. Wherever anything seemed to make a snug fit, I screwed it in. Other remaining things I drove into convenient holes. All the while I begged blind fate to guide me.

LAID UP WITH A BROKEN RUDDER

Then I connected the batteries, supplied the new spark-coil, selected a new spark-plug at random, and screwed it in.

Having done various things, I carefully surveyed my environs for a lady. There were no ladies present, so I spoke out freely. "And now," said I, having exhausted my vocabulary, "I shall crank!"

Bill and the Kid sat on a pile of rocks looking very sullen. For some reason or other they seemed to doubt that engine. I don't know how long I cranked. I know only that the impossible happened. The boat started for the hotel piazza!

I did n't shut her down this time. I leaped out and took her by the nose. Putting our shoulders against the power of the screw, we walked her out into the current, headed her down stream, and scrambled in, wet to the ears.

My logbook speaks for that day as follows: "Left Benton at 2:30 P.M. Gypsied along under half gasoline for several hours, safely crossing the Shonkin and Grocondunez bars. Struck a rock in Fontenelle Rapids at 4:30,

9

taking off rudder. Landed with difficulty on a gravel-bar and repaired damages. At 5:30 engine bucked. A heavy wind from the west beat us against a ragged shore for an hour and a half. Impossible to proceed without power, except by cordelling—which we did, walking waist-deep in the water much of the time. Paddles useless in such a head wind. The wind falling at sunset, we drifted, again losing our rudder while shooting Brule Rapids. Tied up at the head of Black Bluffs Rapids at dusk, having made twenty miles out of two thousand for the first day's run. Have to extend that fifteen days! Just the same, that information bureau saw us leave under power!"

CHAPTER V

WE awoke with light hearts on the second morning of the voyage. All about us was the sacred silence of the wilderness dawn. The coming sun had smitten the chill night air into a ghostly fog that lay upon the valley like a fairy lake.

We were at the rim of the Bad Lands and there were no birds to sing; but crows, wheeling about a sandstone summit, flung doleful voices downward into the morning hush—the spirit of the place grown vocal.

Cloaked with the fog, our breakfast fire of driftwood glowed ruddily. What is there about the tang of wood-smoke in a lonesome place that fills one with glories that seem half memory and half dream? Crouched on my haunches, shivering just enough to feel the beauty there is in fire, I needed only to close my eyes, smarting with the smoke, to feel myself the first man huddled close to the first flame, blooming like a mystic flower in the chill dawn of the world!

Perhaps that is what an outing is for—to strip one down to the lean essentials, press in upon one the glorious privilege of being one's self, unique in all the universe of innumerable unique things. Crouched close to your wilderness campfire, the great Vision comes easily out of the smoke. Once again you feel the bigness of your world, the tremendous significance of everything in it—including yourself—and a far-seeing sadness grips you. Living in the flesh seems so transient, almost a pitiful thing in the last analysis. But somehow you feel that there is something bigger—not beyond it, but all about it continually. And you wonder that you ever hated anyone. You know, somehow, there in the smoky silence, why men are noble or ignoble; why they lie or die for a principle; why they kill, or suffer martyrdom; why they love and hate and fight; why women smile under burdens, sin splendidly or sordidly—and why hearts sometimes break.

And expanded by the bigness of the empty silent spaces about you, like a spirit independent of it and outside of it all, you love the great red straining Heart of Man more than you could ever love it at your desk in town. And you want to get up and move—push on through purple distances—whither? Oh, anywhere will do! What you seek is at the end of the rainbow; it is in the azure of distance; it is just behind the glow of the sunset, and close under the dawn. And the glorious thing about it is that you know you 'll never find it until you reach that lone, ghostly land where the North Star sets, perhaps. You 're merely glad to know that you 're not a vegetable—and that the trail never really ends anywhere.

Just now, however, the longing for the abstract had the semblance of a longing for the concrete. It always has that semblance, for that matter. You never really want what you think you are seeking. Touch the substance—and away you go after the shadow!

Around the bend lay Sioux City.   Around
what   bend?   What   matter?   Somewhere
down   stream   the   last   bend   lay,   and   in
between lay the playing of the game.   Any
bend will do to sail around!   There's a
lot of fun in merely being able to move
about and do things.   For this reason I am
overwhelmed   with   gratitude   whenever   I
think that, through some slight error in the
cosmic process, the life forces that glow in
me might have been flung into a turnip—
but were n't!   The thought is truly appalling
—is n't it?   The avoidance of that one awful
possibility is enough to make any man feel
lucky all his life.   It's such fun to waken in
the morning with all your legs and arms and
eyes and ears about you, waiting to be used
again!   So strong was this thought in me
when we cast off, that even the memory of
Bill's amateurish pancakes could n't keep
back the whistle.

The current of the Black Bluffs Rapids
whisked us from the bank with a giddy speed,
spun us about a right-angled bend, and landed
us in a long quiet lake.   Contrary to the

average opinion, the Upper Missouri is merely a succession of lakes and rapids. In the low-water season, this statement should be itali-cised. When you are pushing down with the power of your arms alone the rapids show you how fast you want to go, and the lakes show you that you can't go that fast. For the teaching of patience, the arrangement is admirable. But when head winds blow, a three-mile reach means about a two-hour fight.

This being a very invigorating morning, however, the engine decided to take a con-stitutional. It ran. Below the mouth of the Marias River, twenty minutes later, we grounded on Archer's Bar and shut down. After dragging her off the gravel, we dis-covered that the engine wished to sleep. No amount of cranking could arouse it. Now and then it would say "*squash*," feebly rolling its wheel a revolution or two—like a sleepy-head brushing off a fly with a languid hand.

A light breeze had sprung up out of the west. The stream ran east and northeast. We hastily rigged a tarp on a pair of oars spliced for a mast, and proceeded at a care-free pace. The light breeze scarcely ruffled the surface of the slow stream;

"—— yet still the sail made on
A pleasant noise till noon."

In the lazy heat of the mounting sun, tempered by the cool river draught, the yellow sandstone bluffs, whimsically decorated with sparse patches of greenery, seemed to waver as though seen through shimmering silken gauze. And over it all was the hush of a dream, except when, in a spasmodic freshening of the breeze, the rude mast creaked and a sleepy watery murmur grew up for a moment at the wake.

Now and then at a break in the bluffs, where a little coulee entered the stream, the gray masses of the bull-berry bushes lifted like smoke, and from them, flame-like, flashed the vivid scarlet of the berry-clusters, smiting the general dreaminess like a haughty cry in a silence.

A wilderness indeed! It seemed that waste land of which Tennyson sang, "where no man

comes nor hath come since the making of the
world." I thought of the steamboats and
the mackinaws and the keel-boats and the
thousands of men who had pushed through
this dream-world and the thought was unconvincing. Fairies may have lived here, indeed;
and in the youth of the world, a glad young
race of gods might have dreamed gloriously
among the yellow crags. But surely we were
the first men who had ever passed that way—
and should be the last.

Suddenly the light breeze boomed up into a
gale. The *Atom*, with bellying sail, leaped
forward down the roughening water, swung
about a bend, raced with a quartering wind
down the next reach, shot across another
bend—and lay drifting in a golden calm.
Still above us the great wind buzzed in the
crags like a swarm of giant bees, and the waters
about us lay like a sheet of flawless glass.

With paddles we pushed on lazily for an
hour. At the next bend, where the river
turned into the west, the great gale that had
been roaring above us, suddenly struck us
full in front. Sucking up river between the

wall rocks on either side, its force was terrific.
You tried to talk while facing it, and it took
your breath away. In a few minutes, in
spite of our efforts with the paddles, we lay
pounding on the shallows of the opposite
shore.

We got out. Two went forward with the
line and the third pushed at the stern. Progress was slow—no more than a mile an hour.
The clear water of the upper river is always
cold, and the great wind chilled the air.
Even under the August noon it took brisk
work to keep one's teeth from chattering.
The bank we were following became a precipice rising sheer from the river's edge, and
the water deepened until we could no longer
wade. We got in and poled on to the next
shallows, often for many minutes at a time
barely holding our own against the stiff
gusts. For two hours we dragged the heavily
laden boat, sometimes walking the bank,
sometimes wading in mid-stream, sometimes
poling, often swimming with the line from
one shallow to another. And the struggle
ended as suddenly as it began. Upon round-

ing the second bend the head wind became a
stern wind, driving us on at a jolly clip until
nightfall.

During the late afternoon, we came upon
a place where the Great Northern Railroad
touches the river for the last time in five
hundred miles. Here we saw two Italian
section hands whiling away their Sunday with
fishing rods. I went ashore, hoping to buy
some fish. Neither of the two could speak
English, and Italian sounds to me merely
like an unintelligible singing. However, they
gave me to understand that the fish were not
for sale, and my proffered coin had no persua-
sive powers.

Still wanting those fish, I rolled a smoke,
carelessly whistling the while a strain from
an opera I had once heard. For some reason
or other that strain had been in my head all
day. I had gotten up in the morning with it;
I had whistled it during the fight with the
head wind. The Kid called it "that Dago
tune." I think it was something from *Il
Trovatore.*

Suddenly one of the little Italians dropped

his rod, stood up to his full height, lifted his arms very much after the manner of an orchestra leader and joined in with me. I stopped—because I saw that he *could* whistle. He carried it on with much expression to the last thin note with all the ache of the world in it. And then he grinned at me.

"Verdi!" he said sweetly.

I applauded. Whereat the little Italian produced a bag of tobacco. We sat down on the rocks and smoked together, holding a wordless but perfectly intelligible conversation of pleasant grins.

That night we had fish for supper! I got them for a song—or, rather, for a whistle. I was fed with more than fish. And I went to sleep that night with a glorious thought for a pillow: Truth expressed as Art is the universal language. One immortal strain from Verdi, poorly whistled in a wilderness, had made a Dago and a Dutchman brothers!

Scarcely had the crackling of the ruddy log lulled us to sleep, when the night had flitted over like a shadow, and we were cooking breakfast. A lone, gray wolf, sitting on his haunches a hundred paces away, regarded us curiously. Doubtless we were new to his generation; for in the evening dusk we had drifted well into the Bad Lands.

Bad Lands? Rather the Land of Awe!

A light stern wind came up with the sun. During the previous evening we had rigged a cat-sail, and noiselessly we glided down the glinting trail of crystal into the "Region of Weir."

On either hand the sandstone cliffs reared their yellow masses against the cloudless sky. Worn by the ebbing floods of a prehistoric sea, carved by the winds and rains of ages, they presented a panorama of wonders.

Rows of huge colonial mansions with pillared porticoes looked from their dizzy terraces across the stream to where soaring mosques and mystic domes of worship caught the sun. It was all like the visible dream of a master architect gone mad. Gaunt, sinister ruins of mediæval castles sprawled down the slopes of unassailable summits. Grim brown towers, haughtily crenellated, scowled defiance on the unappearing foe. Titanic stools of stone dotted barren garden slopes, where surely gods had once strolled in that far time when the stars sang and the moon was young. Dark red walls of regularly laid stone—huge as that the Chinese flung before the advance of the Northern hordes—held imaginary empires asunder. Poised on a dizzy peak, Jove's eagle stared into the eye of the sun, and raised his wings for the flight deferred these many centuries. Kneeling face to face upon a lonesome summit, their hands clasped before them, their backs bent as with the burdens of the race, two women prayed the old, old, woman prayer. The snow-white ruins of a vast cathedral lay along the water's edge, and all about it was a hush of worship. And near it, arose the pointed pipes of a colossal organ—with the summer silence for music.

With a lazy sail we drifted through this place of awe; and for once I had no regrets about that engine. The popping of the exhaust would have seemed sacrilegious in this holy quiet.

Seldom do men pass that way. It is out of the path of the tourist. No excursion steamers ply those awesome river reaches. Across the sacred whiteness of that cathedral's imposing mass, no sign has ever been painted telling you the merits of the best five-cent cigar in the world! Few beside the hawks and the crows would see it, if it were there.

And yet, for all the quiet in this land of wonder, somehow you cannot feel that the place is unpeopled. Surely, you think, invisible knights clash in tourney under those frowning towers. Surely a lovelorn maiden spins at that castle window, weaving her heartache into the magic figures of her loom. Stately dames must move behind the shut doors of those pillared mansions; devotees mutter Oriental prayers beneath those sun-smitten domes. And amid the awful inner silence of that cathedral, white-robed priests lift wan faces to their God.

Under the beat of the high sun the light stern wind fell. The slack sail drooped like a sick-hearted thing. Idly drifting on the slow glassy flood, we seemed only an incidental portion of this dream in which the deepest passions of man were bodied forth in eternal fixity. Towers of battle, domes of prayer, fanes of worship, and then—the kneeling women! Somehow one could n't whistle there. Bill and the Kid, little given to sentiment, sat quietly and stared.

Late in the afternoon we found ourselves out of this "Region of Weir." Great wall rocks soared above us. Consulting our map, we found that we were nearing Eagle Rapids, the first of a turbulent series. I had fondly anticipated shooting them all under power. So once more I decided to go over that engine. We landed at the wooded mouth of a little ravine, having made a trifle over twenty miles that day.

With those tools of the engine doctor— an air of mystery and a monkey-wrench—I unscrewed everything that appeared to have a thread on it, and pulled out the other things. The odds, I figured, were in my favor. A sick engine is useless, and I felt assured of either killing or curing. I did something— I don't know what; but having achieved the complete screwing up and driving in of things —*it went!*

So on the morning of the fourth day, we were up early, eager for the shooting of rapids. We had understood from the conversation of the seemingly wise, that Eagle Rapids was the first of a series that made the other rapids we had passed through look like mere ripples on the surface.   In some of those we had gone at a very good clip, and several times we had lost our rudder.

I remembered how the steamboats used to be obliged to throw out cables and slowly wind themselves up with the power of the "steam nigger." I also remembered the words of Father de Smet: "There are many rapids, ten of which are very difficult to ascend and very dangerous to go down."

We had intended from the very first to get wrecked in one or all of these rapids.   For this reason we had distributed forward, aft, and amidships, eight five-gallon cans, soldered air-tight.   The frail craft would, we figured, be punctured.   The cans would displace nearly three hundred and fifty pounds of water, and the boat and engine, submerged, would lose a certain weight.   I had made the gruesome

10

calculation with fond attention to detail. I decided that she should be wrecked quite arithmetically. We should be able, the figures said, to recover the engine and patch the boat. We had provided three life-preservers, but one had been stolen; so I had fancied what a bully fight one might have if he should be thrown out into the mad waters without a life-preserver.

I have never been able to explain it satisfactorily; it is one of the paradoxes; but human nature seems to take a weird delight in placing in jeopardy that which is dearest. Even a coward with his fingers clenched desperately on the ragged edge of hazard, feels an inexplicable thrill of glory. Having several times been decently scared, I know.

One likes to take a sly peep behind the curtain of the big play, hoping perhaps to get a slight hint as to what machinery hoists the moon, and what sort of contrivance flings the thunder and lightning, and many other things that are none of his business. Only, to be sure, he intends to get away safely with his information. When you think you see your finish bowing to receive you, something happens in your head. It's like a sultry sheet of rapid fire lapping up for a moment the thunder-shaken night—and discovering a strange land to you. And it's really good for you.

Under half speed we cruised through the windless golden morning; and the lonesome canyon echoed and re-echoed with the joyful chortle of the resurrected engine. We had covered about ten miles, when a strange sighing sound grew up about us. It seemed to emanate from the soaring walls of rock. It seemed faint, yet it arose above the din of the explosions, drowned out the droning of the screw.

Steadily the sound increased. Like the ghost of a great wind it moaned and sighed about us. Little by little a new note crept in —a sibilant, metallic note as of a tense sheet of silk drawn rapidly over a thin steel edge.

We knew it to be the mourning voice of the Eagle Rapids; but far as we could see, the river was quiet as a lake. We jogged on for a mile, with the invisible moaning presence about us. It was somewhat like that intangible something you feel about a powerful but sinister personality. The golden morning was saturated with it.

Suddenly, turning a sharp bend about the wall of rock that flanked the channel, a wind of noise struck us. It was like the hissing of innumerable snakes against a tonal background of muffled continuous thunder. A hundred yards before us was Eagle Rapids —a forbidding patch of writhing, whitening water, pricked with the upward thrust of toothlike rocks.

The first sight of it turned the inside of me mist-gray. Temporarily, wrecks and the arithmetic of them had little charm for me. I seized the spark-lever, intending to shut down. Instead, I threw it wide open. With the resulting leap of the craft, all the gray went out of me.

I grasped the rudder ropes and aimed at a point where the sinuous current sucked through a passage in the rocks like a lean flame through a windy flue. Did you ever hear music that made you see purple? It

TYPICAL RAPIDS ON UPPER MISSOURI

was that sort of purple I saw (or did I hear it like music?) when we plunged under full speed into the first suck of the rapids. We seemed a conscious arrow hurled through a gray, writhing world, the light of which was noise. And then, suddenly, the quiet, golden morning flashed back; and we were ripping the placid waters of a lake.

The Kid broke out into boisterous laughter that irritated me strangely: "Where the devil do you suppose our life-preservers are?" he bawled. "They 're clear down under all the cargo!"

A world of wonderful beauty was forging past us. In the golden calm, the scintillant sheet of water seemed to be rushing backward, splitting itself over the prow, like a fabric woven of gold and silver drawn rapidly against a keen stationary blade.

The sheer cliffs had fallen away into pine-clad slopes, and vari-colored rocks flung notes of scarlet and gold through the sombre green of the pines—like the riotous treble cries of an organ pricking the sullen murmur of the bass. So still were the clean waters that we seemed midway between two skies.

We skirted the base of a conical rock that towered three hundred feet above us—a Titan sentinel. It was the famous Sentinel Rock of the old steamboat days. I shut the engine down to quarter speed, for somehow from the dizzy summit a sad dream fell upon me and bade me linger.

I stared down into the cold crystal waters at the base of the rock. Many-colored mosses, sickly green, pale, feverish red, yellow like fear, black like despair, purple like the lips of a strangled man, clung there. I remembered an old spring I used to haunt when I was just old enough to be awed by the fact of life and frightened at the possibility of death. Just such mosses grew in the depths of that spring. I used to stare into it for hours.

It fascinated me in a terrible way. I thought Death looked like that. Even now I am afraid I could not swim long in clear waters with those fearful colors under me. I am sure they found Ophelia floating like a ghastly lily in such a place.

Filled with a shadow of the old childish dread, I looked up to the austere summit of the Sentinel. Scarred and haggard with time it caught the sun. I thought of how long it had stood there just so, under the intermittent flashing of moon and sun and star, since first its flinty peak had pricked through the hot spume of prehistoric seas.

Fantastic reptiles, winged and finned and fanged, had basked upon it—grotesque, tentative vehicles of the Flame of Life! And then these flashed out, and the wild sea fell, and the land arose—hideous and naked, a steaming ooze fetid with gasping life. And all the while this scarred Sentinel stared unmoved. And then a riot of giant vegetation all about it—divinely extravagant, many-colored as fire. And this too flashed out— like the impossible dream of a god too young. And the Great Change came, and the paradox of frost was in the world, stripping life down to the lean essentials till only the sane, capable things might live. And still the Titan stared as in the beginning. And then, men were in the land—gaunt, terrible, wolf-like men, loving and hating. And La Verendrye forged past it; and Lewis and Clark toiled under it through these waters of awful quiet. And then the bull boats and the mackinaws and the packets. And all these flashed out; and still it stood unmoved. And I came—and I too would flash out, and all men after me and all life.

I viewed the colossal watcher with something like terror—the aspect of death about its base and that cynical glimmer of sunlight at its top. I flung the throttle open, and we leaped forward through the river hush. I wanted to get away from this thing that had seen so much of life and cared so little. It depressed me strangely; it thrust a bitter question within the charmed circle of my ego. It gave me an almost morbid desire for speed, as though there were some place I should reach before the terrible question should be answered against me.

We fled down five or six miles of depressingly quiet waters. Once again the wall rocks closed about us. We seemed to be going at a tediously slow pace, yet the two thin

"HOLE-IN-THE-WALL" ROCK ON UPPER MISSOURI

155

streams of water rushed hissing from prow to stern. A strange mood was upon me. Once when I was a boy and far from home, I awoke in the night with a bed of railroad ties under me, and the chill black blanket of the darkness about me. I wanted to get up and run through that damned night— anywhere, just so I went fast enough—stopping only when exhaustion should drag me down. And yet I was afraid of nothing tangible; hunger and the stranger had sharpened whatever blue steel there was in my nature. I was afraid of being still! Were you ever a homesick boy, too proud to tell the truth about it?

I felt something of that boy's ache as we shot in among the wall rocks again. It was a psychic hunger for something that does not exist. Oh, to attain the terrible speed one experiences in a fever-dream, to get somewhere before it is too late, before the black curtain drops!

To some this may sound merely like the grating of overwrought nerves. But it is more than that. All religions grew out of that most human mood. And whenever one is deeply moved, he feels it. For even the most matter-of-fact person of us all has now and then a suspicion that this life is merely episodic—that curtain after curtain of darkness is to be pierced, world after world of consciousness and light to be passed through.

Once more the rocks took on grotesque shapes—utterly ultra-human in their suggestiveness. Those who have marvelled at the Hudson's beauty should drop down this lonesome stretch.

We shot through the Elbow Rapids at the base of the great Hole-in-the-Wall Rock. It was deep and safe—much like an exaggerated mill-race. It ran in heavy swells, yet the day was windless.

In the late afternoon we shot the Dead Man's Rapids, a very turbulent and rocky stretch of water. We went through at a freight-train speed, and began to develop a slight contempt for fast waters. That night we camped at the mouth of the Judith River on the site of the now forgotten Fort Chardon. We had made only ninety-eight

PALISADES OF THE UPPER MISSOURI

miles in four days.   It began to appear that we might be obliged to finish on skates!

We were up and off with the first gray of the morning.   We knew Dauphin Rapids to be about seventeen miles below, and since this particular patch of water had by far the greatest reputation of all the rapids, we were eager to make its acquaintance.

The engine began to show unmistakable signs of getting tired of its job.   Now and then it barked spitefully, had half a notion to stop, changed its mind, ran faster than it should, wheezed and slowed down—acting in an altogether unreasonable way.   But it kept the screw humming nevertheless.

Fortunately it was going at a mad clip when we sighted the Dauphin.   There was not that sibilance and thunder that had turned me a bit gray inside at first sight of the Eagle.   The channel was narrow, and no rocks appeared above the surface.   But speed *was* there; and the almost noiseless rolling of the swift flood ahead had a more formidable appearance than that of the Eagle. Rocks above the surface are not much to be feared when you have power and a good rudder. But we drew about twenty-two inches of water, and I thought of the rocks under the surface.

I had, however, only a moment to think, for we were already travelling a good eighteen miles, and when the main swirl of the rapids seized us, we no doubt reached twenty-five. I was grasping the rudder ropes and we were all grinning a sort of idiotic satisfaction at the amazing spurt of speed, when——

Something was about to happen!

The Kid and I were sitting behind the engine in order to hold her screw down to solid water. Bill, decorated with a grin, sat amidships facing us. I caught a pink flash in the swirl just under our bow, and then *it happened!*

The boat reared like a steeple-chaser taking a fence! The Kid shot forward over the engine and knocked the grin off Bill's face! Clinging desperately to the rudder ropes, I saw, for a brief moment, a good three fourths of the frail craft thrust skyward at an angle of about forty-five degrees. Then she stuck her nose in the water and her screw came up, howling like seven devils in the air behind me! Instinctively, I struck the spark-lever; the howling stopped,—and we were floating in the slow waters below Dauphin Rapids.

All the cargo had forged forward, and the persons of Bill and the Kid were considerably tangled. We laughed loud and long. Then we gathered ourselves up and wondered if she might be taking water under the cargo. It developed that she was n't. But one of our grub boxes, containing all the bacon, was missing. So were the short oars that we used for paddles. While we laughed, these had found some convenient hiding-place.

We had struck a smooth boulder and leaped over it. A boat with the ordinary launch construction would have opened at every seam. The light springy tough construction of the *Atom* had saved her. Whereat I thought of the Information Bureau and was well pleased.

Altogether we looked upon the incident as a purple spot. But we were many miles from available bacon, and when, upon trial, the

engine refused to make a revolution, we began
to get exceedingly hungry for meat.

Having a dead engine and no paddles, we
drifted. We drifted very slowly. The Kid
asked if he might not go ashore and drive a
stake in the bank. For what purpose? Why, to
ascertain whether we were going up or down
stream! While we drifted in the now blistering sun, we talked about *meat*. With a
devilish persistence we quite exhausted the
subject. We discussed the best methods
for making a beefsteak delicious. It made us
very hungry for meat. The Kid announced
that he could feel his backbone sawing at the
front of his shirt. But perhaps that was
only the hyperbole of youth. Bill confessed
that he had once grumbled at his good wife
for serving the steak too rare. He now stated
that at the first telegraph station he would
wire for forgiveness. I advised him to wire
for money instead, and buy meat with it.
Personally I felt a sort of wistful tenderness
for packing-houses.

That day passed somehow, and the next
morning we were still hungry for meat. We

spent most of the morning talking about it. In the blistering windless afternoon, we drifted lazily. Now and then we took turns cranking the engine.

We were going stern foremost and I was cranking. We rounded a bend where the wall rocks sloped back, leaving a narrow arid sagebrush strip along both sides of the stream. I had straightened up to get the kink out of my back and mop the sweat out of my eyes, when I saw something that made my stomach turn a double somersault.

A good eight hundred yards down stream at the point of a gravel-bar, something that looked like and yet unlike a small cluster of drifting, leafless brush moved slowly into the water. Now it appeared quite distinct, and now it seemed that a film of oil all but blotted it out. I blinked my eyes and peered hard through the baffling yellow glare. Then I reached for the rifle and climbed over the gunwale. I smelled raw meat.

Fortunately, we were drifting across a bar, and the slow water came only to my shoulders. The thing eight hundred yards away was forging across stream by this time—heading for the mouth of a coulee. I saw plainly now that the brush grew out of a head. It was a buck with antlers.

Just below the coulee's mouth, the wall rocks began again. The buck would be obliged to land above the wall rocks, and the drifting boat would keep him going. I reached shore and headed for that coulee. The sagebrush concealed me. At the critical moment, I intended to show myself and start him up the steep slope. Thus he would be forced to approach me while fleeing me. When I felt that enough time had passed, I stood up. The buck, shaking himself like a dog, stood against the yellow sandstone at the mouth of the gulch. He saw me, looked back at the drifting boat, and appeared to be undecided.

I wondered what the range might be. Back home in the ploughed field where I frequently plug tin cans at various long ranges, I would have called it six hundred yards—at first. Then suddenly it seemed three or four hundred. Like a thing in a dream the

FRESH MEAT!

buck seemed to waver back and forth in the oily sunlight.

"Call it four hundred and fifty," I said to myself, and let drive. A spurt of yellow stone-dust leaped from the cliff a foot or so above the deer's back. Only four hundred? But the deer had made up his mind. He had urgent business on the other side of that slope—he appeared to be overdue.

I pumped up another shell and drew fine at four hundred. That time his rump quivered for a second as though a great weight had been dropped on it. But he went on with increased speed. Once more I let him have it. That time he lost an antler. He had now reached the summit, two hundred feet up at the least.

He hesitated—seemed to be shivering. I have hunted with a full stomach and brought down game. But there's a difference when you are empty. In that moment before you kill, you became the sort of fellow your mother would n't like. Perhaps the average man would feel a little ashamed to tell the truth about that big savage moment. I got down on my knee and put a final soft-nosed ball where it would do the most good. The buck reared, stiffened, and came down, tumbling over and over.

That night we pitched camp under a lone scrubby tree at the mouth of an arid gulch that led back into the utterly God-forsaken Bad Lands. It was the wilderness indeed. Coyotes howled far away in the night, and diving beaver boomed out in the black stream.

We built half a dozen fires and swung above them the choice portions of our kill. And how we ate—with what glorious appetites!

It is good to sit with a glad-hearted company flinging words of joyful banter across very tall steins. It is good to draw up to a country table at Christmas time with turkey and pumpkin-pies and old-fashioned puddings before you, and the ones you love about you. I have been deeply happy with apples and cider before an open fireplace. I have been present when the brilliant sword-play of wit flashed across a banquet table—and it thrilled me. *But*——

There is no feast like the feast in the open—
the feast in the flaring light of a night fire—
the feast of your own kill, with the tang of the
wild and the tang of the smoke in it!

CHAPTER VI

GETTING DOWN TO BUSINESS

IT all came back there by the smouldering
fires—the wonder and the beauty and the
awe of being alive. We had eaten hugely
—a giant feast. There had been no formali-
ties about that meal. Lying on our blankets
under the smoke-drift, we had cut with our
jack-knives the tender morsels from a haunch
as it roasted. When the haunch was at last
cooked to the bone, only the bone was left.

Heavy with the feast, I lay on my back
watching the gray smoke brush my stars that
seemed so near. *My stars!* Soft and gentle
and mystical! Like a dark-browed Yotun
woman wooing the latent giant in me, the
night pressed down. I closed my eyes, and
through me ran the sensuous surface fires
of her dream-wrought limbs. Upon my face
the weird magnetic lure of ever-nearing, never-

kissing lips made soundless music. Like a sister, like a mother she caressed me, lazy with the giant feast; and yet, a drowsy, half-voluptuous joy shimmered and rippled in my veins.

Drowsing and dreaming under the drifting smoke-wrack, I felt the sense of time and self drop away from me. No now, no to-morrow, no yesterday, no I! Only eternity, one vast whole—sun-shot, star-sprent, love-filled, changeless. And in it all, one spot of consciousness more acute than other spots; and that was the something that had eaten hugely, and that now felt the inward-flung glory of it all; the swooning, half-voluptuous sense of awe and wonder, the rippling, shimmering, universal joy.

And then suddenly and without shock—like the shifting of the wood smoke—the mood veered, and there was nothing but I. Space and eternity were I—vast projections of myself, tingling with my consciousness to the remotest fringe of the outward swinging atom-drift; through immeasurable night, pierced capriciously with shafts of paradoxic day; through and beyond the awful circle of yearless duration, my ego lived and knew itself and thrilled with the glory of being. The slowly revolving Milky Way was only a glory within me; the great woman-star jewelling the summit of a cliff, was only an ecstasy within me; the murmuring of the river out in the dark was only the singing of my heart; and the deep, deep blue of the heavens was only the splendid color of my soul.

Bill snored. Among the glowing fires moved the black bulk of the Kid, turning the hunks of venison. And then the universe and I, curiously mixed, swooned into nothing at all, and I was blinking at a golden glow, and from the river came a shouting.

It was broad day. We leaped up, and rubbing the sleep from our eyes, saw a light skiff drifting toward us. It contained two men—Frank and Charley. We had met them at Benton, and during an acquaintance of three weeks we had learned of their remarkable ability as cooks. Frank was a little Canadian Frenchman, and Charley was English. Both, in the parlance of the road, were "floaters"; that is to say, no locality ever knew them long; the earth was their floor, the sky their ceiling—and their god was Whim. Naturally our trip had appealed to them, and one month in Benton had aggravated that hopelessly incurable disease—*Wanderlust*.

So we had agreed that somewhere down river we would camp for a week and wait for them. They would do the cooking, and we would take them in tow. Two days after we dropped out of Benton, they had abruptly "jumped" an unfinished job and put off after us in a skiff, rowing all day and most of the night in order to overtake us.

Certainly they had arrived at the moment most psychologically favorable for the beginning of an odd sort of tyranny that followed. Cooking is a weird mystery to me. As for Bill and the Kid, courtesy forbids detailed comment. The Kid had been uniformly successful in disguising the most familiar articles of diet; and Bill was perhaps least unsuccessful in the making of flapjacks. According to his naïve statement, he had discovered the

trick of mixing the batter while manufac-
turing photographer's mounting paste. His
statement was never questioned. My only
criticism on his flapjacks was simply that
he left too much to the imagination. For
these and kindred reasons, we gladly hailed
the newcomers.

Ten minutes after the skiff touched shore,
the camp consisted of two cooks and three
scullions. The Kid was a hewer and packer
of wood, I was a pealer and slicer of things,
and Bill, sweetly oblivious of his bewhiskered
dignity, danced about in the humblest of
moods, handing this and that to the grub-
lords.

"You outfitted like greenhorns!" announced
the usurpers. "What you want is raw
material. Run down to the boat, please, and
bring me this! Oh, yes, and bring me that!
And you 'll find the other in the bottom of the
skiff's forward locker! Put a little more wood
on the fire, Kid; and say, Bill, hand me that,
won't you? Who 's going to get a pail of
water?"

All three of us were going to get a pail of

SUPPER!

water, of course! It was the one thing in the world we wanted to do very much—get a pail of water!

But the raw materials—how they played on them! I regarded their performance as a species of duet; and the raw materials, ranged in the sand about the fire, were the keys. Frank touched this, Charley touched that, and over the fire the music grew—perfectly stomach-ravishing!

We had bought with much care all, or nearly all the ordinary cooking-utensils. These the usurpers scorned. Three or four gasoline cans, transformed by a jack-knife into skillets, ovens, platters, etc., sufficed for these masters of their craft. The downright Greek simplicity of their methods won me completely.

"This is indeed Art," thought I; "first, the elimination of the non-essential, and then the virile, unerring directness, the seemingly easy accomplishment resulting from effort long forgotten; and, above all, the final, convincing delivery of the goods."

Out of the chaos of the raw material, beneath the touch of Charley's wise hands, emerged a wondrous cosmos of biscuits, light as the heart of a boy. And Frank, singing a French ditty, created wheat cakes. His method struck me as poetic. He scorned the ordinary uninspired cook's manner of turning the half-baked cake. One side being done, he waited until the ditty reached a certain lilting upward leap in the refrain, when, with a dexterous movement of the frying-pan, he tossed the cake into the air, making it execute a joyful somersault, and catching it with a sizzling *splat* in the pan, just as the lilting measure ceased abruptly.

Why, I could taste that song in the pancakes!

I wonder why domestic economy has so persistently overlooked the value of song as an adjunct to cookery. *Gâteaux à la chansonnette!* Who would n't eat them for breakfast?

At six in the evening we put off, Charley, the Kid, and I manning the power boat, Bill and Frank the skiff, which was towed by a thirty-foot line. I had, during the day, transformed my unquestioned slavery into a distinct advantage, having carefully impressed

upon the Englishman the honor I would do
him by allowing him to become chief engineer
of the *Atom*.   I carefully avoided the subject
of cranking.   I was tired cranking.   I felt
that I had exhausted the possibilities of enjoy-
ment in that particular form of physical
exercise.   It had developed during the day
that Charley had once run a gasoline engine.
I was careful to emphasize my ridiculous lack
of mechanical ability.   Charley took the
bait beautifully.

But just now the engine ran merrily.
Above its barking I sang the praises of the
Englishman, with a comfortable feeling that,
at least in this, the tail would wag the
dog.

Through the clear quiet waters, between
soaring canyon walls, we raced eastward into
the creeping twilight.   Here and there the
banks widened out into valleys of wondrous
beauty, flanked by jagged miniature mountains transfigured in the slant evening light.
It seemed the "færie land forlorn" of which
Keats dreamed, where year after year come
only the winds and the rains and the snow

and the sunlight and the star-sheen and the moon-glow.

In the deepening evening our widening V-shaped wake glowed with opalescent witch-fires. Watching the oily ripples, I steered wild and lost the channel. We all got out and, wading in different directions, went hunting for the Missouri River. It had flattened out into a lake three or four hundred yards wide and eight inches deep. Slipping poles under the power boat, we carried it several hundred yards to a point where the stream deepened. It was now quite dark, and the engine quit work for the day. The skiff towed us another mile or so to a camping place.

Having moored the boats, we lined up on the shore and had a song. It was a quintet, consisting of a Frenchman, an Englishman, an Irishman, a Cornishman, and a German. A very strong quintet it was; that is to say, strong on volume. As to quality—we were n't thrusting ourselves upon an audience. The river and the sky did n't seem to mind, and, the cliffs sang after us, lagging a beat or two.

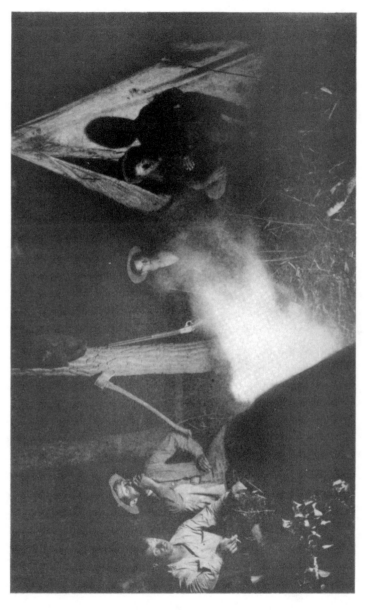

NIGHT IN CAMP

183

We wished to sing ever so beautifully; and, after all, it would be much better to have the whole world wishing to sing melodiously, than to have just a few masters here and there who really can! Did you ever hear a barefooted, freckle-faced ploughboy singing powerfully and quite out of tune, the stubble fields about him still glistening with the morning dew, and the meadow larks joining in from the fence-posts? I have: and soaring above the faulty execution, I heard the lark-heart of the never-aging world wooing the far-off eternal dawn. True song is merely a hopeful condition of the soul. And so I am sure we sang very wonderfully that night.

And how the flapjacks disappeared as a result of that singing! We ate until Charley refused to bake any more; then we rolled up in our blankets by the fire and "swapped lies," dropping off one at a time into sleep until the last speaker finished his story with only the drowsy stars for an audience. At least I suppose it was so; I was not the last speaker.

Alas! too seldom were we to hail the even-

ing star with song. So far we had made in a
week little more than one hundred and fifty
miles. With the exception of a few hours of
head winds, that week had been a week of
dream. We now awoke fully to the fact that
in low water season the Missouri is not swift.
In our early plans we had fallen in with the
popular fallacy that one need only cut loose
and let the current do the rest; whereas, in
low water, one would probably never reach
the end of his journey by that method. In
addition to this, our gasoline was running low.
We had trusted to irrigation plants for
replenishing our supply from time to time.
But the great flood of the spring had swept
the valley clean. Where the year before
there were prosperous ranch establishments
with gasoline pumping plants, there was only
desolation now. It was as though we travelled in the path of a devastating army.
Perhaps the summer of 1908 was the most
unfavorable season for such a trip in the last
fifty years. Steamboating on the upper river
is only a memory. There are now no wood-
yards as formerly. We found ourselves with

no certainty of procuring grub and oil; our
engine became more and more untrust-
worthy; our paddles had been lost. What
winds we had generally blew against us, and
the character of the banks was changing.
The cliffs gave way to broad alluvial valleys,
over which, at times, the gales swept with
terrific force.

Our map told us of a number of river
"towns." We had already been partially
disillusioned as to the character of those
"towns." They were pretty much in a class
with Goodale, except that they lacked the
switch and the box-car and the sign. Just
now Rocky Point lay ahead of us. Rocky
Point meant a new supply of food and oil.
Stimulated by this thought, Charley cranked
heroically under the blistering sun and managed to arouse the engine now and then into
spasms of speed. He had not yet begun to
swear. Fearfully I awaited the first evidence
of the new mood, which I knew must come.

At least once a day we put the machinery
on the operating table. Each time we succeeded only in developing new symptoms.

At a point about fifty miles from the "town" so deeply longed for, a lone cow-punch appeared on the bank.

"How far to Rocky Point?" I cried.

"Oh, something less than two hundred miles!" drawled the horseman. (How carelessly they juggle with miles in that big country!)

"It's just a little place, isn't it?" I continued.

"Little place!" answered the cow-punch; "hell, no!"

"What!" I cried in glee; "Is it really a town of importance?" I had visions of a budding metropolis, full of gasoline and grub.

"I guess it ain't a little place," explained the rider; "*w'y, they've got nigh onto ten thousand cattle down there!*"

Ten minutes after that, Charley, after a desperate but unsuccessful fit of cranking, straightened the kink out of his back, mopped the perspiration from his face—*and swore!*

Almost immediately I felt, or at least thought I felt, a distinct change in the temper of the crew—for the worse. We used the

WOLF POINT, THE FIRST TOWN IN FIVE HUNDRED MILES

189

better part of two days covering the last fifty miles into Rocky Point, only to find that the place consisted of a log ranch-house, two women, an old man, and "Texas." The cattle and the other men were scattered over a hundred miles or so of range. The women either would not or could not supply us with grub, explaining that the nearest railroad town was ninety miles away. Gasoline was out of the question. We might be able to buy some at the mouth of Milk River, *two hundred miles down stream!*

"Texas," who made me think of Gargantua, and who had a chest like a bison bull's, and a drawling fog-horn voice, ran a saloon in an odd little shanty boat brought down by the flood. He solved the problem for us.

"You cain't get no gasoline short o' Milk River," he bellowed drawlingly; "and you sure got to paddle, so you better buy whiskey!"

While we were deciding to accept the offered advice, "Texas" whittled a stick and got off a few jokes of Rabelaisian directness. We laughed heartily, and as a mark of his appreciation, he gave us five quarts for a gallon. Which proved, in spite of his appearance, that "Texas" was very human.

We gave the engine a final trial. It ran by spasms—backwards. Then, finally, it refused to run at all. We tried to make ourselves believe that the gasoline was too low in the tank, that the pressure of the oil had something to do with it. At first we really knew better. But days of drudgery at the paddles transformed the makeshift hope into something almost like a certainty.

There was no lumber at Rocky Point. We rummaged through a pile of driftwood and found some half-rotted two-by-sixes. These we hacked into paddles. They weighed, when thoroughly soaked, at least fifteen pounds apiece.

Sending Bill and Frank on ahead with the skiff and the small store of provisions, Charley and I, the Kid at the steering rope, set out pushing the power canoe with the paddles. The skiff was very soon out of sight.

The *Atom*, very fast under power, was, with paddles, the slowest boat imaginable.

There was no lift to her prow, no exhilarating leap as with the typical light canoe driven by regulation paddles. And she was as unwiedly as a log. A light wind blew up-stream, and the current was very slow. After dark we caught up with Bill and Frank, who had supper waiting. I had been tasting venison all day; but there was none for supper. In spite of a night's smoking, all of it had spoiled. This left us without meat. Our provisions now consisted mostly of flour. We had a few potatoes and some toasted wind called "breakfast food." During six or seven hours of hard work at the paddles, we had covered no more than fifteen miles. These facts put together gave no promising result. In addition to this, it was impossible to stir up a song. Even the liquor would n't bring it out. And the flapjacks were not served *à la chansonnette* that night. I tried to explain why the trip was only beginning to get interesting; but my words fell flat. And when the irrepressible Kid essayed a joke, I alone laughed at it, though rather out of gratitude than mirth.

13

There are many men who live and die with the undisputed reputation of being good fellows—your friends and mine—who, if put to the test, would fail miserably. Fortunate is that man to whom it is not given to test all of his friends. This is not cynicism; it is only human nature; and I love human nature, being myself possessed of so much of it. I admire it when it stands firmly upon its legs, and I love it when it wobbles. But when it gains power with increasing odds, grows big with obstacles, I worship it.

" To thrill with the joy of girded men,
    To go on forever and fail, and go on again—
    With the half of a broken hope for a pillow at night—"

Thus it should have been. But that night, staring into the faces of three of the four, I saw the yellow streak. The Kid was not one of the three. The first railroad station would hold out no temptation to him. He was a kid, but manhood has little to do with age. It must exist from the first like a tang of iron in the blood. Age does not really create anything—it only develops. Your wonderful

NIGHT ON THE UPPER MISSOURI

and beautiful things often come as paradoxes. I looked for a man and found him in
a boy.

Bill talked about home and stared into the
twilight. The "floaters" were irritable, quar-
re'ling with the fire, the grub, the cooking-
utensils, and verbally sending the engine to
the devil.

Seeing about eighteen hundred miles of
paddle work ahead, knowing that at that
season of the year the prevailing winds would
be head winds, and having very little faith in
the engine under any conditions, I decided
to travel day and night, for the water was
falling steadily and already the channels were
at times hard to find. Charley and Frank
grumbled. I told them we would split the
grub fairly, a fifth to a man, and that they
might travel as slowly as they liked, the skiff
being their property. They stayed with us.

We lashed the boats together and put off
into the slow current. A haggard, eerie
fragment of moon slinked westward. Stars
glinted in the flawless chilly blue. The surface of the river was like polished ebony—a

dream-path wrought of gloom and gleam. The banks were lines of dusk, except where some lone cottonwood loomed skyward like a giant ghost clothed with a mantle that glistered and darkled in the chill star-sheen.

There was the feel of moving in eternity about it all. The very limitation of the dusk gave the feeling of immensity. There was no sense of motion, yet we moved. The sky seemed as much below as above. We seemed suspended in a hollow globe. Now and then the boom of a diving beaver's tail accented the clinging quiet; and by fits the drowsy muttering of waterfowl awoke in the adjacent swamps, and droned back into the universal hush.

Frank and I stood watch, the three others rolling up in their blankets among the luggage. It occurred to me for the first time that we had a phonograph under the cargo. I went down after it. At random I chose a record and set the machine going. It was a Chopin *Nocturne* played on a 'cello—a vocal yearning, a wailing of frustrate aspirations, a brushing of sick wings across the gates of heavens never to be entered; and then the finale—an insistent, feverish repetition of the human ache, ceasing as with utter exhaustion.

I looked about me drinking in the night. How little this music really expressed it! It seemed too humanly near-sighted, too egotistic, too petty to sound out under those far-seeing stars, in that divine quiet.

I slipped on another record. This time it was a beautiful little song, full of the sweet melancholy of love. I shut it down. The thing would n't do. In the evening—yes. But *now!* Truly there is something womanly about Night, something loverlike in a vast impersonal way; but too big—she is too terribly big to woo with human sentiment. Only a windlike chant would do—something with an undertone of human despair, out-soared by brave, savage flights of invincible soul-hope—great virile singing man-cries, winged as the starlight, weird as space— Whitman sublimated, David's soul poured out in symphony.

I started another going. This time I did not stop it, for the Night was singing—

—through its nose perhaps, but still it was singing—out of that machine. It was Wagner's *Evening Star* played by an orchestra. It filled the night, swept the glittering reaches, groped about in the glooms; and then, leaving the human theme behind, soul-like the upward yearning violins took flight, dissolving at last into starlight and immensity. Ages swept by me like a dream-wind. When I got back, the machine, all but run down, was scratching hideously.

Slowly we swung about in the scarcely perceptible current. Down among the luggage the three snored discordantly. Frank's cigarette glowed intermittently against the dim horizon, like a bonfire far off. Somewhere out in the gloom coyotes chattered and yelped, and from far across the dusky valley others answered—a doleful tenson.

I dozed. Frank awoke us all with a shout. We leaped up and stared blinkingly into the north. That whole region of the sky was aflame from zenith to horizon with spectral fires. It was the aurora. Not the pale, ragged glow, sputtering like the ghost of a huge lamp-flame, which is familiar to every one, but a billowing of color, rainbows gone mad! In the northeast the long rolling columns formed—many-colored clouds of spectral light whipped up as by a whirlwind—flung from eastward to westward, devouring Polaris and the Wain—rapid sequent towers of smokeless fire!

It dazzled and whirled and mounted and fell like the illumined filmy skirts of some invisible Titanic serpentine dancer, madly pirouetting across a carpet of stars. Then suddenly it all fell into a dull ember-glow and flashed out. The ragged moon dropped out of the southwestern sky. In the chill of the night, gray, dense fog wraiths crawled upon the hidden face of the waters.

Again I dozed and awakened with the sense of having stopped suddenly. A light wind had arisen and we were fast on a bar. Frank and I took our blankets out on the sand, rolled up and went to sleep.

The red of dawn awoke us as though some one had shouted. Frank and I sat up and stared about. A white-tail deer was drinking at the river's edge three hundred yards away. So far as we were concerned, it was a dream-deer. We blinked complacently at it until it disappeared in the brush. Then we thought of the rifle.

We were all stiff and chilled. The boats were motionless in shallow water. We all got out in the stream that felt icy to us, and waded the crafts into the channel. Incidentally we remembered Texas and his wisdom.

The time was early August; but nevertheless there was a tang of frost in the air and the river seemed to flow not water but a thick frore fog. I smelled persimmons distinctly—it was that cold; brown spicy persimmons smashed on crisp autumn leaves down in old Missouri! The smell haunted me all morning like a bitter-sweet regret.

We breakfasted on flapjacks and, separating the boats, put off. The skiff left us easily and disappeared. A head wind arose with the sun and increased steadily. By eleven o'clock it blew so strongly that we could make no headway with the rude paddles, and the waves, rolling at least four feet from trough to crest, made it impossible to hold the boat in course. We quit paddling, and got out in the water with the line. Two pulled and one pushed. All day we waded, sometimes up to our necks; sometimes we swam a bit, and sometimes we clung to the boat and kicked it on to the next shallows. Our progress was ridiculously slow, but we kept moving. When we stopped for a few minutes to smoke under the lee of a bank, our legs cramped.

To lay up one day would be only to establish a precedent for day after day of inactivity. The prevailing winds would be head winds. We clung to the shoddy hope held out by that magic name—Milk River. We knew too well that Milk River was only a snare and a delusion; but one must fight toward something—it makes little difference what you call that something. A goal, in itself, is an empty thing; all the virtue lies in the moving toward the goal.

Often we sank deep in the mud; often at the bends we could scarcely forge against the blast that held us leaning to the pull. Noon came and still we had not overtaken the skiff. Dark came, and we had not yet sighted it. But with the sun, the wind fell, and we paddled on, lank and chilled. About ten o'clock we sighted the campfire.

We ate flapjacks once more—delicious, butterless flapjacks!—and then once more we put off into the chill night. We made twelve miles that day, and every foot had been a fight. I wanted to raise it to twenty-five before sunrise. No one grumbled this time; but in the light of the campfire the faces looked cheerless—except the Kid's face.

We huddled up in our blankets and, naturally, all of us went to sleep. A great shock brought us to our feet. The moon had set and the sky was overcast. Thick night clung around us. We saw nothing, but by the rocking of the boats and the roaring of the river, we knew we were shooting rapids.

Still dazed with sleep, I had a curious sense of being whirled at a terrific speed into some subterranean suck of waters. There was nothing to do but wait. We struck rocks and went rolling, shipping buckets of water at every dip. Then there was a long sickening swoop through utter blackness. It ended abruptly with a thud that knocked us down.

We found that we were no longer moving. We got out, hanging to the gunwales. The boats were lodged on a reef of rock, and we were obliged to "walk" them for some distance, when suddenly the water deepened, and we all went up to our necks. And the night seemed bitterly cold. I never shivered more in January.

It was yet too dark to find a camping place; so we drifted on until the east paled. Then we built a great log fire and baked ourselves until sunrise.

Day after day my log-book begins with the words, "Heavy head winds," and ends with "Drifted most of the night." We covered about twenty-five miles every twenty-four hours. Every day the cooks grumbled more; and Bill had a way of staring wistfully into the distance and talking about home, that produced in me an odd mixture of anger and pity.

We had lost our map: we had no calendar. Time and distance, curiously confused, were merely a weariness in the shoulders.

CHAPTER VII

ON TO THE YELLOWSTONE

AT last one evening (shall I confess it?) we had blue-crane soup for supper!

Now a flight of gray-blue cranes across a pearl-gray sky, shot with threads of evening scarlet, makes a masterly picture: indeed, an effect worthy of reproduction in Art. You see a Japanese screen done in heroic size; and it is a sight to make you long exquisitely for things that are not—like a poet. But——

Let us have no illusions about this matter! Crane soup is not satisfactory. It looks gray-blue and tastes gray-blue, and gives to your psychic inwardness a dull, gray-blue, melancholy tone. And when you nibble at the boiled gray-blue meat of an adult crane, you catch yourself wondering just what sort of *ragout* could be made out of boots; you have a morbid longing to know just how bad such a *ragout* would really be!

Hereafter on whatever trails I may follow, blue cranes shall be used chiefly for Japanese screen effects.   Little by little (the latent philosopher in me emerges to remark) by experience we place not only ourselves but all things in their proper places in the universe.   This process of fitting things properly in one's cosmos seems to be one of the chief aims of conscious life.   Therefore I score one for myself—having placed blue cranes permanently in that cosmic nook given over to Japanese screen effects!

Next morning we pushed on.   The taste of that crane soup clung to me all day like the memory of an old sorrow dulled by time.

Deer tracks were plentiful, but it has long been conceded that the tracks are by far the least edible things pertaining to an animal. Cranes seemed to have multiplied rapidly. Impudently tame, they lined the gravel-bars, and regarded us curiously as we fought our way past them.   Now and then a flock of wild ducks alighted several hundred yards from us. We had only a rifle. To shoot a moving duck out of a moving boat with a rifle is a feat attended with some difficulties. Once we wounded a wild goose, but it got away; which offended our sense of poetic justice. After crane soup one would seem to deserve roast goose.

I scanned the dreary monotonous valleys stretching away from the river. We had for several days been living on scenery, tobacco, and flapjacks. The scenery had flattened out, tobacco was running low; but the flapjacks bid fair to go on forever. I sought in my head for the exact adjective, the particular epithet with the inevitable feel about it, with which to describe that monotonous melancholy stretch. Every time I tried, I came back to the word "*baconless*." The word took on exquisite overtones of gray meaning, and I worked up those overtones until I had a perfectly wrought melancholy poem of one word—"*Baconless*." For, after all, a poem never existed upon paper, but lives subtly in the consciousness of the poet, and in the minds of those who understand the poet

14

through the suggestiveness of his written symbols, and their own remembered experiences.

But during the next morning, poetic justice worked. A rider mounted on a piebald pony appeared on the bank and shouted for us to pull in.

I suddenly realized why a dog wags his tail at a stranger. But the feeling I had was bigger than that. This mounted man became at once for me the incarnation of the meaning of bacon!

When two parties meet and each wants what the other can give, it does n't take long to get acquainted. The rider was a youth of about seventeen. One glance at his face told you the story of his rearing. He was unmistakably city-bred, and his hands showed that his life had begun too easy for his own good.

"From the East?" he questioned joyously. "Say, you know little old New York, don't you? When were you there last?"

The lad was hungry, but not for bacon. Alas! Our hunger was the healthier one!

We talked of New York. "Mother's in Paris," he volunteered, "and Dad's in New York meeting her bills. But the Old Man's got a grouch at me, and so he sent me 'way out here in this God-forsaken country! Say, what did they make this country for? Got any tailor-made cigarettes about you? How did Broadway look when you were there last? Lights all there yet at night? I've been here two years—it seems like two hundred! Talk about Robinson Crusoe! Say, I've got him distanced!"

I helped him build up a momentary Broadway there in the wilderness—the lights, the din, the hurrying, jostling theatre crowds, the cafés, faces, faces—anguished faces, eager faces, weary faces, painted faces, squalor, brilliance. For me the memory of it only made me feel the pity of it all. But the lad's eyes beamed. He was homesick for Broadway.

I changed the subject from prose to poetry; that is, from Broadway to bacon.

"Wait here till I come back," said the lad, mounting. He spurred up a gulch and disappeared. In an hour he reappeared with a half strip of the precious stuff. "Take money for it? Not on your life!" he insisted. "You 've been down there, and that goes for a meal ticket with me!"

Fried bacon! And flapjacks sopped in the grease of it! After all, a banquet is very much a state of mind.

When we pulled away, the ostracized New Yorker bade us farewell with a snatch of a song once more or less popular: "Give my regards to Broadway!"

We pushed on vigorously now. The head wind came up. *The head wind!* It seemed one of the eternal things. We paddled and cordelled valiantly, discussing Milk River the while. We had grown very credulous on that subject. Somehow or other an unlimited supply of gasoline was all the engine needed for the complete restoration of its health; and Milk River stood for gasoline in liberal quantities. Hope is generally represented by the poets as a thing winged and ethereal; nevertheless it can be fed on bacon.

The next morning we arrived at the mouth

ENTRANCE TO THE BAD LANDS

of what we took to be Hell Creek, which flows (when it has any water in it!) out of the Bad Lands. It did n't take much imagination to name that creek. The whole country from which it debouches looks like Hell— "with the lights out," as General Sully once remarked. A country of lifeless hills that had the appearance of an endless succession of huge black cinder heaps from prehistoric fires.

The wind had increased steadily all day, and now we saw ahead of us a long rolling stretch of wind-lashed river that discouraged us somewhat. A gray mist rolled with the wind, and dull clouds scudded over. We pitched camp in a clump of cottonwoods and made flapjacks; after which the Kid and I, taking our blankets and the rifle, set out to explore Hell Creek.

The windings of the ravine soon hid us from the river, and we found ourselves in a melancholy world, without life and without any human significance. It was very easy to imagine one's self lost amid the drear ashen craters of the moon. We pushed on up the creek, kicking up clouds of alkali dust as we went.   A creek of a burnt-out hell it was, to be sure.   It seemed almost blasphemous to call this arid gully a creek.   Boys swim in creeks, and fishes twinkle over the shallows where the sweet eager waters make a merry sound.   Creek, indeed!   Did a cynic name this dry ragged gash in the midst of a bleak black world where nothing lived, where never laughter sounded?

A seething, fiery ooze might have flowed there once, but surely never did water make music there.

We pushed on five or six miles, and the evening shade began to press in about us.   At last we issued forth into a flat basin, surrounded by the weird hills—a grotesque, wind-carved amphitheatre, admirably suited for a witches' orgy.   Some bleached bison heads with horns lay scattered about the place, and a cluster of soapweeds grew there— God knows how!   They thrust their sere yellow sword-blades skyward with the pitiful defiance of desperate things.   It seemed natural enough that something should be dead in this sepulchre; but the living weeds,

"WALKING" BOATS OVER SHALLOWS

fighting bitterly for life, seemed out of place.

I looked about and thought of Poe.   Surely just beyond those summits where the melancholy sky touched the melancholy hills, one would come upon the "dank tarn of Auber" and the "ghoul-haunted woodland of Weir."

We gathered a quantity of the dry sword-bladed soapweeds, and with one of the blankets made a lean-to shelter against the steep hillside.   The place was becoming eerie in the gray evening that spread slowly over the dead land.   The mist driven by the moaning wind became a melancholy drizzle. We dragged the soapweeds under cover and lit a fire with difficulty.   It was a half-hearted, smudgy, cheerless fire.

And then the night fell—tremendous, over-powering night!   The Kid and I, huddled close in one blanket, thrust our heads out from under the shelter and watched the ghastly world leap by fits out of the dark, when the sheet lightning flared through the drizzle.   It gave one an odd shivery feeling.

It was as though one groped about a strange dark room and saw, for a brief moment in the spurting glow of a wind-blown sulphur match, the staring face of a dead man. Over us the great wind groaned. Water dripped through the blanket—like tears. We scraped the last damp ends of the weeds together that the fire might live a little longer. Byron's poem came back to me with a new force; and lying on my stomach in the cheerless drip before a drowning fire, I chanted snatches of it aloud to the Kid and to that sinister personality that was the Night.

> I had a dream which was not all a dream;
> The bright sun was extinguished, and the stars
> Did wander darkling in eternal space,
> Rayless and pathless; and the icy earth
> Swung blind and blackening in the moonless air.

Low thunder shook the ink-sopped night— I thought of it as the Spirit of Byron applauding his own terrific lines.

> A fearful hope was all the world contained;
> Forests were set on fire—but hour by hour
> They fell and faded—and the crackling trunks
> Extinguished with a crash—and all was black.

REVEILLE!

Out in the wind-voiced darkness, swept by spasmodic deluges of rapid flame and muffled thunder, it seemed I could hear the dream-forests of the moody Master crackling and booming in the gloom.

> —looked up
> With mad disquietude on the dull sky,
> The pall of a past world.

" Say, how long is that piece ? " asked the Kid.

> And vipers crawled
> And twined themselves among the multitude,
> Hissing—

We wondered if there might not be some rattlesnakes in that vicinity.

—They raked up
And shivering, scraped with their cold skeleton hands
The feeble ashes, and their feeble breath
Blew for a little life, and made a flame
Which was a mockery; then they lifted up
Their eyes as it grew brighter, and beheld
Each other's aspects—saw and shrieked and died—

"Cut that out!" said the Kid.
"Why?" I asked.

"Because," said the Kid.

But what are Bad Lands for? I had hoped to chant a bit of James Thomson, the younger, also, there in that "dreadful night." I never was in a place where it seemed to fit so well.

But we huddled up in our blanket under the dripping shelter, and I gave myself over to a downright, almost wickedly primitive feeling. We slept some—but that was a rather long night. The soppy gray morning came at length. A midsummer morning after a night of rain—and yet, no bird, no hopeful greenery, no sense of the upward yearning Earth-Soul!

When we sighted the Missouri River again, the sun had broken through upon the greengirt, glinting stream. It seemed like Paradise.

By almost continuous travel we reached Lismus Ferry on the second morning from Hell Creek. The ferryman had a bit of information for us. We would find nothing at the mouth of Milk River but a sandbar, he advised us. But he had some ointment to apply to the wound thus inflicted, in that

"ATOM" SAILING UP-STREAM IN A HEAD-WIND

Glasgow, a town on the Great Northern, was only twenty-five miles inland. The weekly stage had left on the morning before; but the ferryman understood that the trail was not overcrowded with pedestrians.

It was a smarting ointment to apply to so fresh a wound; but we took the medicine. Frank, Charley, and I set out at once for Glasgow, leaving the others at camp to repair the leaking boat during our absence. The stage trail led through an arid, undulating prairie of yellow buffalo grass. There were creek beds, but they were filled with dust at this season of the year. The Englishman set the pace with the stride of the long-legged. The sun rose high; the dry runs reminded us unpleasantly of our increasing thirst, and the puffing wind blew hot as from a distant prairie fire.

I followed at the Englishman's heels, and by and by it began to occur to me that he could walk rather rapidly. The Frenchman trailed after at a steadily increasing distance, until finally I could no longer hear his forceful remarks (uttered in two languages) concerning a certain corn which he possessed. We had been cramped up in a boat for several weeks, and the frequent soakings in the cold water had done little good to our joints. None of us was fit for walking. I kept back a limp until the Englishman ahead of me began to step with a little jerking of the knees; and then with an almost vicious delight, I gave over and limped. I never knew before the great luxury of limping. We covered the distance in something less than six hours.

The next morning, in a drizzling rain, each packing a five-gallon can of gasoline and some provisions, we set out for the Ferry; and it was a sorry, bedraggled trio that limped up to camp eight hours later. We did little more than creep the last five miles. And all for a spiteful little engine that might prove ungrateful in the end!

It rained all night—a cold, insistent downpour. Our log fire was drowned out; the tent dripped steadily; our blankets got soppy; and three of us were so stiff that the least movement gave keen pain.

TYPICAL UPPER MISSOURI RIVER REACH

229

Soppy dawn—wet wood—bad grub for breakfast—and bad humor concealed with difficulty; but through it all ran a faint note of victory at the thought of the gasoline, and the way that engine would go! We lay in camp all day—soppy, sore—waiting for the rain to let up. By way of cheering up I read *L'Assomoir;* and a grim graveyard substitute for cheer it was. But the next day broke with a windy, golden dawn. We filled the tank, packed the luggage and lo! the engine worked! It took all the soreness out of our legs to see it go.

We rejoiced now in the heavy and steadily increasing head wind; for it was like conquering an old enemy to go crashing through the rolling water that had for so many days given us pitiless battle.

For five or six miles we plunged on down the wind-tumbled river. There was a distinct change in the temper of the crew. A vote at that time would have been unanimous for finishing at New Orleans.

Squash!

The engine stopped; the *Atom* swung round

in the trough of the waves, and the tow-skiff rammed us, trying to climb over our gunwale. We wallowed in the wash of a bar, and cranked by turns. At the end of an hour no illusions were left us. Holding an inquest over the engine, we pronounced it dead.

In the drear fag end of the windy day, soaked from much wading and weary of paddling with little headway, we made camp in a clump of scarlet bull-berry bushes; and by the evening fire two talked of railroad stations, one talked of home, and I thought of that one of the "soldiers three" who "swore quietly into the sky."

The Milk River illusion was lost. Two hundred miles below was the mouth of the Yellowstone—the first station in the long journey. A few days back we had longed for gasoline; but there was no one to sell. Now we had fifteen gallons to sell—and there was no one to buy. The hope without the gasoline was decidedly better than the gasoline without the hope. Whereat the philosopher in me emerges to remark—but who cares? Philosophy proceeds backward, and

A STRING OF ASSINIBOINE PEARLS!

points out errors of thought and action chiefly
when it has become too late to mend them.
But it is possible to be poor in the possession
of erstwhile prospective wealth, and rich in
retrospective poverty. Oh, blessed is he
who is negatively rich!

Being a bit stunned by the death of the hope
conceived in weariness, we did not put off
that night, but huddled up in our blankets
close to the log fire; for this midsummer night
had in it a tang of frost.

Day came—cloudy and cold—blown over
the wilderness by a wind that made the
cottonwoods above us groan and pop. The
waves were higher than we had seen them
before. We had little heart for cordelling,
and no paddling could make headway against
that gale. It was Sunday. Everything was
damp and chilly. Shivers ran up our backs
while we toasted our feet and faces; and the
wind-whipt smoke had a way of blowing in
every direction at once. Charley struggled
with the engine, which now and then made
a few revolutions—backwards—by way of
leading him on. He heaped big curses upon

it, and it replied periodically with snorts of rage.

Bad blood developed, and mutiny ensued, which once gave promise of pirate-story developments—fortunately warded off. Before the day was done, it was made plain that the Kid and I would travel alone from the mouth of the Yellowstone. "For," said the Kid with certain virile decorations of speech, "I'm going with you if we have to buy skates!"

The wind fell at sunset. A chill, moonless, starry night lured me, and I decided to travel. The mutineers, eager to reach a railroad as soon as possible, agreed to go. The skiff led and the *Atom* followed with paddles. A mile or so below we ran into shallows and grounded. We waded far around in the cold water that chilled us to the marrow, but could find neither entrance nor outlet to the pocket in which we found ourselves. Wading ashore, we made a cheerless camp in the brush, leaving the boats stuck in the shallows. For the first time, the division in the camp was well marked. The Kid and I instinctively made our bed

ASSINIBOINE INDIAN CHIEF

together under one blanket, and the others bunked apart. We had become the main party of the expedition; the others were now merely enforced camp followers. It was funny in an unpleasant way.

In the morning a sea of stiff fog hid our boats. Packing the camp stuff on our backs, we waded about and found the crafts.

At last, after a number of cheerless days and nights of continuous travel, the great, open, rolling prairies ahead of us indicated our approach toward the end of the journey's first stage. The country began to look like North Dakota, though we were still nearly two hundred miles away. The monotony of the landscape was depressing. It seemed a thousand miles to the sunrise. The horizon was merely a blue haze—and the endless land was sere. The river ran for days with a succession of regularly occurring right-angled bends to the north and east. Each headland shot out in the same way, with, it seemed, the same snags in the water under it, and the same cottonwoods growing on it; and opposite each headland was the same stony bluff, wind- and water-carved in the same way: until at last we cried out against the tediousness of the oft-repeated story, wondering whether or not we were continually passing the same point, and somehow slipping back to pass it again.

But at last we reached Wolf Point—the first town in five hundred miles. We had seen no town since we left Benton. An odd little burlesque of a town it was; but walking up its main street we felt very metropolitan after weeks on those lonesome river stretches.

Five Assiniboine Indian girls seemed to be the only women in the town. I coaxed them to stand for a photograph on the incontestable grounds that they were by far the prettiest women I had seen for many days! The effect of my generous praise is fixed forever on the pictured faces presented herewith.

Here, during the day, Frank and Charley disposed of their skiff and we saw them no more. We pushed on with little mourning. But in a spirit of fairness, let me record that Charley's biscuits were marvels, and that

ASSINIBOINE INDIAN CAMP

241

Frank's *gâteaux à la chansonnette* were things of beauty and therefore joys forever.

The days that followed were long and hard; and half the chilly nights were spent in drying ourselves before a roaring fire. There were more mosquitoes now. They began to torture us at about five o'clock in the afternoon, and left off only when the cold of night came, relieving us of one discomfort by the substitution of another. Bill, of whom I had come to think as the expatriated turnip, gave me an opportunity to study homesickness—at once pitiful and ludicrous in a man with abundant whiskers. But he pulled strenuously at the forward paddle, every stroke, as he remarked often, taking him closer to home.

The river had fallen alarmingly, and was still falling. Several times we were obliged to unload the entire cargo, piling it high in the shallow water, that we might be able to carry the empty boat to the channel.

One evening we came upon a typical Montana ranch—the Pen and Key. The residence, barns, sheds, fences were built of logs. The great rolling country about it was thickly dotted with horses and cattle. The place looked like home. It was a sight from Pisgah—a glimpse of a Promised Land after the Wilderness. We pulled in, intending to buy some provisions for the last stage of the journey to the Yellowstone.

I went up to the main ranch-house, and was met at the door by one of those blessed creatures that have "mother" written all over them. Hers were not the eyes of a stranger. She looked at me as she must look at one of her sons when he returns from an extended absence. I told at once the purpose of my errand, explaining briefly what we were doing on the river. Why, yes, certainly we could have provisions. But we were n't going any farther that night—were we? The rancher appeared at this moment— a retired major of the army, who looked the part—and decided that we would stay for supper. How many were there in our party? Three? "Three more plates," he said to the daughters of the house, busy about the kitchen.

Let 's be frank! It really required no per-

THE PEN AND KEY RANCH

245

suasion at all to make a guest of me. Had I
allowed myself adequate expression of my
delight, I should have startled the good
mother by turning a somersault or a series
of cartwheels! Oh, the smell of an old-
fashioned wholesome meal in process of
development!

A short while back I sang the praises of the
feast in the open—the feast of your own kill,
tanged with the wood smoke. And even
here I cling to the statement that of all meals,
the feast of wild meat in the wilderness takes
precedence. But the supper we ate that
evening takes close second. Welcome on
every face!—the sort of welcome that the
most lavish tips could not buy. And after
the dishes were cleared away, they brought
out a phonograph, and we all sat round like
one family, swapping information and yarns
even up, while the music went on. When we
left next morning at sunrise, it seemed that
we were leaving home—and the river reaches
looked a bit dismal all that day.

Having once been a vagabond in a non-
professional way, I have a theory about

the physiognomy of houses. Some have a forbidding, sick-the-dog-on-you aspect about them, not at all due, I am sure, to architectural design. Experience has taught me to be suspicious of such houses. Some houses have the appearance of death—their windows strike you as eyeless sockets, the doors look like mouths that cannot speak. The great houses along Fifth Avenue seemed like that to me. I could walk past them in the night and feel like a ghost. I have seen cottages that I wanted to kneel to; and I 'm sure this feeling was n't due to the vine growing over the porch or the roses nodding in the yard. Knock at the door of such a house, and the chances are in favor of your being met by a quiet, motherly woman—one who will instantly make you think of your own mother. Some very well constructed houses look surly, and some shabby ones look kind, somehow. If you have ever been a book agent or a tramp, how you will revel in this seeming digression! God grant that no man in need may ever look wistfully at your house or at mine, and pass on with a shake of the head.

It is a subtle compliment to have book agents and tramps frequently at one's door.

Am I really digressing? My theme is a trip on a great river. Well, kindness and nature are not so far apart, let us believe.

Now this ranch-house looked hospitable; there was no mistaking it. Wherefore I deduce that the spirit of the inhabitants must pierce through and emanate from the senseless walls like an effluvium. Who knows but that every house has its telltale aura, plain to a vision of sufficient spiritual keenness? Perhaps some one will some day write a book *On the Physio-Psychological Aspect of Houses :* and there will be an advance sale of at least one copy on that book.

At noon on the fourth day from the Pen and Key Ranch, we pulled up at the Mondak landing two miles above the mouth of the Yellowstone. We were thoroughly soaked, having dragged the boat the last two or three miles through the shallows and intermittent deeps of an inside channel. The outer channel was rolling viciously in that eternal thing, the head wind. We had covered the first six hundred miles with a power boat (called so, doubtless, because it required so much power to shove it along!) in a little less than four weeks. During that time we had received no mail, and I was making a break for the post-office, oozing and feeling like an animated sponge, when a great wind-like voice roared above me: *"Hey there!"*

I looked up to the hurricane deck of a steamer that lay at the bank taking on freight. A large elderly man, dressed like a farmer, with an exaggerated straw hat shading a face that gripped my attention at once, was looking down at me. It was the face of a born commander; it struck me that I should like to have it cast in bronze to look at whenever a vacillating mood might seize me.

"Come aboard!" bawled the man under the ample hat. There was nothing in the world just then that I wished for more than my mail; but somehow I felt the will to obey— even the necessity of obeying.

"You came from Benton?" he asked, when I had clambered up the forward companion-

251 ON THE HURRICANE DECK OF THE "EXPANSION"; CAPT. MARSH THIRD FROM THE LEFT

way and stood dripping before the captain of
the steamer *Expansion*.   At this closer range,
the strength of the face was even more impres-
sive, with its eagle beak and its lines of firm-
ness; but a light of kindness was shed through
it, and the eyes took on a gentle expression.

"How did you find the water?"

"Very low, sir; we cordelled much of the
way."

"I tried to get this boat to Benton," he said,
"and got hung up on the rocks above Lismus
Ferry."

"And we drifted over them helter-skelter
at midnight!"

He smiled, and we were friends.   Thus I
met Captain Grant Marsh, the Grand Old
Man of the Missouri River.   He was freight-
ing supplies up the Yellowstone for the great
Crane Creek irrigation dam, sixty miles above
the mouth.   The *Expansion* was to sail on the
following day, and I was invited to go along.
Seeing that the Captain was short of help,
I insisted upon enlisting as a deck hand for
the trip.

It was work, very hard work.   I think I

should prefer hod-carrying as a profession, for we had a heavy cargo, ranging from lumber and tiling to flour and beer; and there are no docks on the Yellowstone. The banks were steep, the sun was very hot, and the cargo had to be landed by man power. My companions in toil swore bitterly about everything in general and steamboating in particular.

"How much are you getting?" asked a young Dane of me, as we trudged up the plank together.

"Nothing at all," I said.

He swore an oath of wonder, and stopped to look me over carefully for the loose screw in my make-up.

"—nothing but the fun of it," I added.

He sniffed and looked bewildered.

"Did it ever occur to you," said I, "that a man will do for nothing what he would n't do for money?"

I could see my conundrum playing peek-a-boo all about his stolid features. After that the Dane treated me with an air of superiority—the superiority of thirty dollars per month over nothing at all.

CRANE CREEK IRRIGATION DAM, UP THE YELLOWSTONE RIVER

We stopped twice to coal, and worked far
into the night. There are no coal chutes on
the Yellowstone. We carried and wheeled
the stuff aboard from a pile on the bank.
During a brief interval of rest, the young
Dane announced to the others that I was
working for nothing; whereat questioning eyes
were turned upon me in the dull lantern light;
whereupon I thought of the world-old mutual
misunderstanding between the proletaire and
the dreamer. And I said to myself: I can
conceive of heaven only as an improbable condition in which all men would be willing and
able to work for nothing at all. I had read
in the Dane's face the meaning of a price.
Heaving coal, I built Utopias.

When the boat was under way, I sat in
the pilot-house with the Captain, watching
the yellow flood and the yellow cliffs drift
past like a vision. And little by little, this
old man who has followed the river for over
sixty years, pieced out the wonderful story
of his life—a story fit for Homer. That story
may now be read in a book, so I need not tell
it here. But I came to think of him as the

incarnation of the river's mighty spirit; and I am proud that I served him as a deck hand.

As we steamed out of the Yellowstone into the clear waters of the Missouri, the Captain pointed out to me the spot upon which Fort Union stood. Upon landing, I went there and found two heaps of stone at the opposite corners of a rectangle traced by a shallow ditch where of old the walls stood. This was all that remained of the powerful fort— virtually the capital of the American Fur Company's Upper Missouri empire—where Mackenzie ruled—Mackenzie who was called King!

Long slough grass grew there, and blue waxen flowers struggled up amid the rubble of what were once defiant bastions. I lay down in the luxuriant grass, closed my eyes, and longed for a vision of heroic days. I thought of the Prince who had been entertained there with his great retinue; of the regality of the haughty Scotchman who ruled there; of Alexander Harvey, who had killed his enemy on the very spot, doubtless, where I lay: killed him as an outraged brave man

kills—face to face before the world.   I thought
of Bourbonais, the golden-haired Paris of this
fallen Ilium.   I thought of the plague that
raged there in '37, and of Larpenteur and his
friend, grim, jesting carters of the dead!

It all passed before me—the unwritten
Iliad of a stronghold forgotten. But the
vision would n't come. The river wind
moaned through the grasses.

I looked off a half-mile to the modern town
of Mondak, and wondered how many in that
town cared about this spot where so much
had happened, and where the grass grew so
very tall now.

I gathered blue flowers and quoted, with
a slight change, the lines of Stevenson:

> But ah, how deep the grass
> Along the battlefield!

CHAPTER VIII

DOWN FROM THE YELLOWSTONE

THE geographer tells us that the mouth of the Missouri is about seventeen miles above St. Louis, and that the mouth of the Yellowstone is near Buford, North Dakota. It appeared to me that the fact is inverted. The Missouri's mouth is near Buford, and the Yellowstone empties directly into the Mississippi!

I find that I am not alone in this opinion. Father de Smet and other early travellers felt the truth of it; and Captain Marsh, who has piloted river craft through every navigable foot of the entire system of rivers, having sailed the Missouri within sound of the Falls and the Yellowstone above Pompey's Pillar, feels that the Yellowstone is the main stem and the Missouri a tributary.

Where the two rivers join, even at low

water, the Yellowstone pours a vast turbulent flood, compared with which the clear and quieter Missouri appears an overgrown rain-water creek. The Mississippi after some miles obliterates all traces of its great western tributary; but the Missouri at Buford is entirely lost in the Yellowstone within a few hundred yards. All of the unique character-istics by which the Missouri River is known are given to it by the Yellowstone—its tur-bulence, its tawniness, its feline treachery, its giant caprices.

Examine closely, and everything will take on before your eyes either masculine or feminine traits. Gender, in a broad sense, is universal, and nothing was created neuter. The Upper Missouri is decidedly female: an Amazon, to be sure, but nevertheless not a man. Beautiful, she is, alluring or terrible, but always womanlike. But when you strike the ragged curdling line of muddy water where the Yellowstone comes in, it is all changed. You feel the sinewy, nervous might of the man.

So it is, that when you look upon the Mis-

souri at Kansas City, it is the Yellowstone
that you behold!

But names are idle sounds; and being of a
peace-loving disposition, I would rather with-
draw my contention than seriously disturb
the geographical *status quo!* Let it be said
that the Upper Missouri is the mother and
the Yellowstone the father of this turbulent
Titan, who inherits his father's might and
wonder, and takes through courtesy the
maiden name of his mother. There! I am
quite appeased, and the geographers may
retain their nomenclature.

At Mondak, Luck stood bowing to receive
us. The *Atom I* had suffered more from con-
tact with snags and rocks than we had supposed. For several hundred miles her intake
of water had steadily increased. We had
toiled at the paddles with the water half-way
to our knees much of the time; though now
and then—by spasms—we bailed her dry.
She had become a floating lump of discourage-
ment, and still fourteen hundred miles lay
ahead.

But on the day previous to our sailing, a

STEAMBOAT "EXPANSION" ON THE YELLOWSTONE

nervous little man with a wistful eye offered us a trade. He had a steel boat, eighteen feet long, forty inches beam, which he had built in the hours between work and sleep during the greater part of a year.

His boat was some miles up the Yellowstone, but he spoke of her in so artless and loving a manner—as a true workman might speak— and with such a wistful eye cast upon our boat, that I believed in him and his boat. He had no engine. It was the engine in our boat that attracted him, as he wished to make a hunting trip up river in the fall. He stated that his boat would float, that it was a dry boat, that it would row with considerable ease. "Then," said I, "paddle her down to the mouth of the Yellowstone, and the deal is made." After dark he returned to our camp with a motor boat, ready to take us to our new craft, *Atom II*.

Leaving all our impedimenta to be shipped by rail, that is, Bill, the tent, extra blankets, phonograph—everything but a few cooking-utensils, an axe, a tarp, and a pair of blankets —the Kid and I got in with the little man and dropped down to the Yellowstone. The new boat was moored under a mud bank. I climbed in, lit a match, and my heart leaped with joy. She was staunch and beautiful—a work of love, which means a work of honesty. Fore and aft were air-tight compartments. She had an oil tank, a water tank, engine housing, steering wheel, lockers. She was ready for the very engine I had ordered to be shipped to me at Bismarck. She was dry as a bone, and broad enough to make a snug bed for two.

The little man and the motor boat dropped out into the gloom and left us gloating over our new possession, sending thankful rings of tobacco smoke at the stars. When the first flush of triumph had passed, we rolled up in the bottom of the boat, lulled to sleep by the cooing of the fusing rivers, united under our gunwale. Such a sleep—a *dry* sleep! and the sides of the boat protected us against the chill night wind.

And the dawn came—shouting merrily like a boy! I once had a chum who had a habit of whistling me out of bed now and then of a

FORT UNION IN 1837

(From a painting by Bödmer)

summer morning, when the birds were just awakening, and the dew looked like frost on the grass. And the sun that morning made me think of my old boy chum with his blithe, persistent whistling. For the first hard stage of the journey was done; all had left me but a brave lad who would take his share of the hardships with a light heart. (All boys are instinctively true sportsmen!) And before us lay the great winding stretch of a savage river that I had loved long—the real Missouri of my boyhood.

A new spirit had come upon us with the possession of the *Atom II*—the spirit of the forced march. For nearly a month we had floundered, trusting to a sick engine and inefficient paddles. Now we had a staunch, dry boat, and eight-foot oars. We trusted only ourselves, and we were one in the desire to push the crooked yellow miles behind us. During the entire fourteen hundred miles that desire increased, until our progress was little more than a retreat. We pitched no camps; we halted only when we could proceed no further owing to sandbars encountered in the dark; we ate as we found it convenient to do so. Regularly relieving each other at the oars, one sat at the steering wheel, feeling for the channel. And it was not long until I began to note a remarkable change in the muscles of the Kid, for we toiled naked to the waist most of the time. His muscles had shown little more than a girl's when we first swam together at Benton. Now they began to stand out, clearly defined, those of his chest sprawling rigidly downward to the lean ribs, and little eloquent knots developed on the bronzed surface of his once smooth arms. He was at the age of change, and he was growing into a man before my eyes. It was good to see.

All the first day the gods breathed gently upon us, and we made fifty miles, passing Trenton and Williston before dark. But the following day, our old enemy, the head wind, came with the dawn. We were now sailing a river more than twice the size of the Upper Missouri, and the waves were in proportion. Each at an oar, with the steering wheel lashed, we forged on slowly but steadily. In mid-

SITE OF OLD FORT UNION

stream we found it impossible to control the boat, and though we hugged the shore whenever possible, we were obliged to cross with the channel at every bend. When the waves caught us broadside, we were treated to many a compulsory bath, and our clothes were thoroughly washed without being removed. An ordinary skiff would have capsized early in the day, but the *Atom II* could carry a full cargo of water and still float.

By sunset the wind fell, the river smoothed as a wrinkled brow at the touch of peace. Aided by a fair current, we skulled along in the hush of evening through a land of vast green pastures with "cattle upon a thousand hills." The great wind had spread the heavens with ever deepening clouds. The last reflected light of the sun fell red upon the burnished surface of the water. It seemed we were sailing a river of liquified red flame; only for a short distance about us was the water of that peculiar Missouri hue which makes one think of bad coffee colored with condensed milk.

Slowly the colors changed, until we were

in the midst of a stream of iridescent opal fires; and quite lost in the gorgeous spectacle, at length we found ourselves upon a bar.

We got out and waded around in water scarcely to our ankles, feeling for a channel. The sand was hard; the bar seemed to extend across the entire river; but a thin rippling line some fifty yards ahead told us where it ended. We found it impossible to push the heavy boat over the shallows. The clouds were deepening, and the night was coming rapidly. Setting the Kid to work digging with an oar at the prow, I pushed and wriggled the stern until I saw galaxies. Thus alternately digging and pushing, we at last reached navigable depths.

It was now quite dark. Low thunder was rolling, and now and then vivid flashes of lightning discovered the moaning river to us— ghastly and forbidding in the momentary glare. We decided to pull in for the night; but in what direction should we pull? A drizzling rain had begun to fall, and the sheet lightning glaring through it only confused us—more than the sooty darkness that show-

ered in upon us after the rapid flashes. We
sat still and waited. In the intermittent
silences, the rain hissed on the surface of the
river like a shower of innumerable heated
pebbles. Ahead of us we heard the dull
booming of the cut banks, as the current
undermined ponderous ledges of sand.

Now, a boat that happens under a falling
cut bank, passes at once into the region of forgotten things. The boat would follow the
main current; the main current flows always
under the cut banks. How long would it
take us to get there? Which way should we
pull? Put a simpler question: In which way
were we moving? We had n't the least
conception of direction. For us the night had
only one dimension—*out !*

Finally a great booming and splashing
sounded to our left, and the boat rocked
violently a moment after. We grasped the
oars and pulled blindly in what we supposed
to be the opposite direction, only to be met
by another roar of falling sand from that
quarter.

There seemed to be nothing to do but have

faith in that divinity which is said to superintend the goings and comings of fools and drunkards. Therefore we abandoned the oars, twiddled our thumbs, and let her drift. We could n't even smoke, for the rain was now coming down merrily. The Kid thought it a great lark, and laughed boisterously at our predicament. By flashes I saw the drenched grin under his dripping nose. But for me, some lines written by that sinister genius, Wainwright, came back with a new force, and clamored to be spoken:

" *Darkness—sooty, portentous darkness— shrouds the whole scene; as if through a horrid rift in a murky ceiling, a rainy deluge— 'sleety flaw, discolored water '—streams down amain, spreading a grisly spectral light, even more horrible than that palpable night.*"

At length the sensation of sudden stopping dizzied us momentarily. We thrust out an oar and felt a slowly sloping bar. Driving the oar half-way into the soft sand, we wrapped the boat's chain about it and went to bed, flinging the tarp over us.

A raw dawn wind sprinkled a cheerless

morning over us, and we got up with our joints grinding rustily.   We were in the midst of a desolate waste of sand and water.   The bar upon which we had lodged was utterly bare.   Drinking a can of condensed milk between us, we pushed on.

That day we found ourselves in the country of red barns.   It was like warming cold hands before an open grate to look upon them.   At noon we saw the first wheat-field of the trip—an undulating golden flood, dimpled with the tripping feet of the wind. These were two joys—quite enough for one day.   But in the afternoon the third came— the first golden-rod.   My first impulse was to take off my hat to it, offer it my hand.

That evening we pulled up to a great bank, black-veined with outcrops of coal, and cooked supper over a civilized fire.   For many miles along the river in North Dakota, as well as along the Yellowstone in Montana, these coal outcrops are in evidence.   Doubt-less, within another generation, vast mining operations will be opened up in these localities. Coal barges will be loaded at the mines and dropped down stream to the nearest railroad point.

We were in the midst of an idyllic country—green, sloping, lawn-like pastures, dotted sparsely with grotesque scrub oaks. Far over these the distant hills lifted in filmy blue. The bluffs along the water's edge were streaked with black and red and yellow, their colors deepened by the recent rains. Lazy with a liberal supper, we drifted idly and gave ourselves over for a few minutes to the spell of this twilight dreamland. I stared hard upon this scene that would have delighted Theocritus; and with little effort, I placed a half-naked shepherd boy under the umbrella top of that scrub oak away up yonder on the lawny slope. With his knees huddled to his chin, I saw him, his fresh cheeks bulged with the breath of music. I heard his pipe—clear, dream-softened—the silent music of my own heart. Dream flocks sprawled tinkling up the hills.

With a wild burst of scarlet, the sunset flashed out. Black clouds darkened the visible idyll. A chill gust swept across stream,

showering rain and darkness. Each at an
oar, we forged on, until we lost the channel in
the gloom. At the first peep of day we were
off again, after a breakfast of pancakes,
bacon, and coffee.

We were gradually becoming accustomed
to the strain of constant rowing. For at
least sixteen hours a day we fought the wind,
during which time the oars were constantly
dipping; and very often our day lengthened
out to twenty hours. We had no time-piece,
and a night of drifting was divided into two
watches. These watches we determined
either by the dropping of a star toward the
horizon, or by the position of the moon when
it shone. On dark nights, the sleeper trusted
to the judgment of his friend to call when the
watch seemed sufficiently long. Daily the
water fell, and every inch of fall increased
the difficulty of travelling.

We were now passing through the country
of the Mandans, Gros Ventres, and Ricarees,
the country through which old Hugh Glass
crawled his hundred miles with only hate to
sustain him. To the west lay the barren

lands of the Little Missouri, through which
Sully pushed with his military expedition
against the Sioux on the Yellowstone. An
army flung boldly through a dead land—a
land without forage, and waterless—a laby-
rinth of dry ravines and ghastly hills! Sully
called it "hell with the lights out." A magnificent, Quixotic expedition that succeeded!
I compared it with the ancient expeditions—
and I felt the eagle's wings strain within me.
Sully! There were trumpets and purple
banners for me in the sound of the name!

Late in the evening we reached the mouth
of the Little Missouri. There we found one
of the few remaining mud lodges of the ancient type. We landed and found ourselves
in the midst of a forsaken little frontier town.
A shambling shack bore the legend, "Store,"
with the "S" looking backward—perhaps
toward dead municipal hopes. A few tumble-
down frame and log shanties sprawled up the
desultory grass-grown main street, at one end
of which dwelt a Mandan Indian family in
the mud lodge.

A dozen curs from the lodge resented our

intrusion with canine vituperation. I thrust
my head into the log-cased entrance of the
circular house of mud, and was greeted with
a sound scolding in the Mandan jargon,
delivered by a squaw of at least eighty years.
She arose from the fire that burned in the
centre of the great circular room, and approached me with an "I-want-your-scalp"
expression. One of her daughters, a girl
dressed in a caricature of the white girl's gar-
ments, said to me: "She wants to know what
you 've got to trade." To this old woman
of the prairie, all white men were traders.

"I want to buy," I said, "eggs, meat,
bread, anything to eat."

The old woman looked me over with a
whimper of amused superiority, and disappeared, soon reappearing with a dark brown
object not wholly unlike a loaf of bread.
"Wahtoo," she remarked, pointing to the
dark brown substance.

I gave her a half-dollar. Very quietly she
took it and went back to her fire. "But,"
said I, "do you sell your bread for fifty cents
per loaf?"

The girl giggled, and the old woman gave me another piece of her Mandan mind. She had no change, it appeared. I then insisted upon taking the balance in eggs. The old woman said she had no eggs. I pointed to a flock of hens that was holding a sort of woman's club convention in the yard, discussing the esthetics of egg-laying, doubtless, while neglecting their nests.

The old lady arose majestically, disappeared again, and reappeared with three eggs. I protested. The Mandan lady forthwith explained (or at least it appeared so to me) all the execrable points in my character. They seemed to be numerous, and she appeared to be very frank about the matter. My moral condition, apparently, was clearly defined in her own mind. I withdrew in haste, fearing that the daughter at any moment might begin to translate.

We dropped down river a few miles, prepared supper, and attacked the dark brown substance which the Indian lady had called "wahtoo." At the first bite, I began to learn the Mandan tongue. I swallowed a

chunk whole, and then enlightened the Kid
as to a portion of the Mandan language.
"Wahtoo," said I, "means 'indigestible'; it is
an evident fact." Then, being strengthened
by our linguistic triumph, we fell upon the
dark brown substance again. But almost
anything has its good points; and I can
conscientiously recommend Mandan bread
for durability!

Once more we had a rainy night. The
tarp, stretched across the boat, sagged with
the water it caught, and poured little persistent streams upon us. The chief of these
streams, from point of size, seemed con-
sciously aiming at my ear. Thrice I turned
over, shifted my position; thrice I was awakened by the sound of a merry brooklet pouring
into that persecuted member.

Somewhere in the world the white cock
was crowing sleepily when we put off, stiff
and soaked and shivering.

Early in the day the fine sand from banks
and bars began to lift in the wind. It
smarted our faces like little whip lashes.
Very often we could see no further than a

hundred and fifty yards in any direction. Only by a constant, rapid dipping of the oars could the boat be held perpendicular to the choppy waves. One stroke missed meant hard work for both of us in getting out of the trough.

Fighting every foot of water, we wallowed through the swells—past Elbow Woods, past Fort Berthold, past the forlorn, raggedy little town, "Expansion." (We rechristened it "Contraction"!)

During the day the gale swept the sky clear. The evening air was crisp and invigorating. We cooked supper early and rowed on silently over the mirroring waters, between two vast sheets of stars, through a semilucent immensity. Far ahead of us a high cliff loomed black and huge against the spangled blue-black velvet of the sky. On its summit a dark mass soared higher. We thought it a tree, but surely a gigantic one. Approaching it, the soaring mass became a medieval castle sitting haughtily with frowning crenellations upon an impregnable rock; and the Missouri became for the moment a

DEAPOLIS, N. D., THE SITE OF OLD FORT CLARK

larger Rhine. At last, rowing up under the
sheer cliff, the castle resolved itself into a
huge grain elevator, its base a hundred feet
above the stream.

Although it was late, we tied our boat,
clambered up a zigzag path, and found ourselves in one of the oddest little towns in the
West—Manhaven—one of the few remaining
steamboat towns.

The main street zigzagged carelessly
through a jumble of little houses. One light
in all the street designated the social centre of
the town, so we went there. It was the
grocery store—a general emporium of ideas
and canned goods.

Entering, we found ourselves in the midst
of "the rustic cackle of the burg." I am sure
the municipal convention was verbally re-
constructing the universe; but upon our entrance, the matter was abruptly laid on the
table. When we withdrew, the entire convention, including the groceryman, adjourned,
and accompanied us to the river where the
general merits of our boat were thoroughly
discussed by lantern light. Also, various

conflicting versions of the distance to Bismarck were given—each party being certain of his own infallibility.

There is something curious about the average man's conception of distance. During the entire trip we found no two men who agreed on this general subject. After acquiring a book of river distances, we created much amusement for ourselves by asking questions. The conversation very often proceeded in this manner:

"Will you please tell us how far it is to So-and-So?"

"One hundred and fifty-two and a half miles!" (with an air of absolute certainty).

"But you are slightly mistaken, sir; the exact distance is sixty-two and seven tenths miles!" (Consternation on the face of the omniscient informant.)

Once a man told us that a certain town was one hundred and fifty miles down stream. We reached the town in an hour and a half!

Information and advice are the two things in this world that the average man will give gladly; and in ninety-nine cases out of a

WASHBURN, N. D.

possible hundred, he is mistaken.   I am convinced that in most cases there is no lying
intent.   A curious chapter could be written on
"The Psychology of Information and Advice."

However, we had more success with the
Indian.   On day we came upon an old Mandan buck and squaw, who were taking a bath
in the river, doubtless feeling convinced that
they needed it.   The current took us within
fifty yards of them.   Upon our approach,
they got out of the water and sat in the sand,
quite as nude and unashamed as our much
abused first parents before the apple ripened.

"Bismarck—how far?" I shouted, standing
up in the boat.

The buck arose in all his unclothed dignity,
raised his two hands, shut and opened them
seven times, after which he lowered one arm,
and again opened and shut a hand.   Then
with a spear-like thrust of the arm toward the
southeast, he stiffened the index finger in the
direction of Bismarck. He meant "seventy-
five miles as the crow flies."   As near as I
could figure it out afterward, he was doubtless correct.

At noon the next day we reached the mouth of the Knife River, near which stood the Mandan village made famous by Lewis and Clark as their winter quarters. Fort Clark also stood here. Nothing remains of the Fort but the name and a few slight indentations in the ground. A modern steamboat town, Deapolis, occupies the site of the old post. Across the river there are still to be seen the remains of trenches. A farmer pointed them out to us as all that remains of the winter camp of the great explorers.

In the late evening we passed Washburn, the "steamboat centre" of the upper river, fifty water miles from Bismarck. It made a very pretty appearance with its neat houses climbing the hillside. Along the water front, under the elevators, a half-dozen steamboats of the good old-fashioned type, lay waiting for their cargoes. Two more boats were building on the ways.

Night caught us some five miles below the town, and, wrapping ourselves in our blankets, we set to drifting. I went on watch and the Kid rolled up forward and went to sleep.

THE LANDING AT BISMARCK, N. D.

After sixteen hours of rowing in the wind, it is a difficult matter to keep awake. The night was very calm; the quiet waters crooned sleepily about the boat. I set myself the task of watching the new moon dip toward the dim hills; I intended to keep myself awake in that manner. The moon seemed to have stuck. Slowly I passed into an impossible world, in which, with drowsy will, I struggled against an exasperating moon that had somehow gotten itself tangled in star-sheen and could n't go down.

I awoke with a start. My head was hanging over the gunwale—the dawn was breaking through the night wall. A chill wind was rolling breakers upon us, and we were fast upon a bar. I awakened the Kid and we put off. We had no idea of the distance covered while sleeping. It must have been at least twenty miles, for, against a heavy wind, we reached Bismarck at one o'clock.

We had covered about three hundred and fifty miles in six days, but we had paid well for every mile. As we passed under the Bismarck bridge, we confessed that we were thoroughly fagged. It was the thought of the engine awaiting us at this town that had kept us from confessing weariness before.

I landed and made for the express office three miles away. A half-hour later I stood, covered with humility and perspiration, in the awful presence of the expressman, who regarded me with that lofty "God-and-I" air, characteristic of some emperors and almost all railroad officials. I stated to the august personage that I was looking for an engine shipped to me by express.

It seems that my statement was insulting. The man snarled and shook his head. I have since thought that he was the owner of the Northern Pacific system in disguise. I suggested that the personage might look about. The personage could n't stoop to that; but a clerk who overheard my insulting remark (he had not yet become the owner of a vast transportation system) condescended to make a desultory search. He succeeded in digging up a spark-coil—and that is all I ever saw of the engine.

During my waiting at Bismarck, I had a

BOATS LAID UP FOR THE WINTER AT WASHBURN, N. D.

talk with Captain Baker, manager of the Benton Packet Line. We agreed in regard to the Government's neglect of duty toward the country's most important natural thoroughfare, the Missouri River. Above Sioux City, the Government operates a snag-boat, the *Mandan*, at an expense ridiculously disproportionate to its usefulness. The *Mandan* is little more than an excursion boat maintained for a few who are paid for indulging in the excursions. A crew of several hundred men with shovels, picks, and dynamite, could do more good during one low water season than such boats could do during their entire existence.

The value of the great river as an avenue of commerce is steadily increasing; and those who discourage the idea of "reopening" navigation of the river, are either railroad men or persons entirely ignorant of the geography of the Northwest. Captain Marsh would say, "Reopen navigation? I 've sailed the river sixty years, and in that time navigation has not ceased."

Rocks could and should be removed from

the various rapids, and the banks at certain points should be protected against further cutting. A natural canal, extending from New Orleans in the South and Cincinnati in the East to the Rockies in the Northwest, is not to be neglected long by an intelligent Government.

As a slow freight thoroughfare, this vast natural system of waterways is unequalled on the globe. Within another generation, doubtless, this all-but-forgotten fact will be generally rediscovered.

Having waited four days for the engine, we put off again with oars. It was near sundown when we started, hungry for those thousand miles that remained. When we had pulled in to the landing at Bismarck, we were like boxers who stagger to their corners all but whipped. But we had breathed, and were ready for another round. A kind of impersonal anger at the failure of another hope nerved us; and this new fighting spirit was like another man at the oars. Many of the hard days that followed left on our memories little more than the impress of a

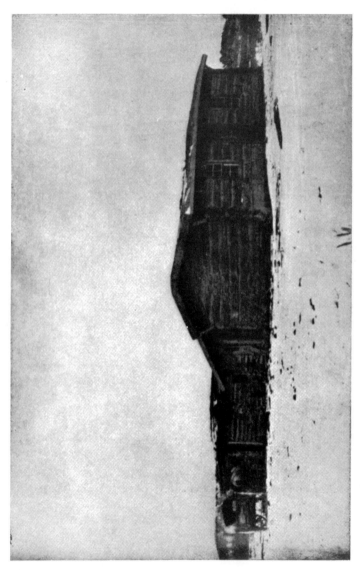

301   ROOSEVELT'S RANCH-HOUSE; NOW IN POSSESSION OF THE NORTH DAKOTA HIST. SOCIETY AT BISMARCK

troubled dream. We developed a sort of contempt for our old enemy, the head wind—that tireless, intangible giant that lashed us with whips of sand, drove us into shallows, set its mighty shoulders against our prow, roared with laughter at us when, soaked and weary, we walked and pushed our boat for miles at a time. The quitter that is in all men more or less, often whispered to us when we were weariest: "Why not take the train? What is it all for?" Well, what is life for? We were expressing ourselves out there on the windy river. The wind said we could n't, and our muscles said we should n't, and the snag-boat captain had said we could n't get down—so we went on. We were now in full retreat—retreat from the possibility of quitting.

During the first night out, an odd circumstance befell us that, for some hours, seemed likely to lose us our boat. As usual, we set to drifting at dark. The moon, close on its half, was flying, pale and frightened, through scudding clouds. However, the wind blew high, and the surface of the water was unruffled. There could be nothing more eerie than a night of drifting on the Missouri, with a ghastly moon dodging in and out among the clouds. The strange glimmer, peculiar to the surface of the tawny river at night, gives it a forbidding aspect, and you seem surrounded by a murmuring immensity.

We were, presumably, drifting into a great sandy bend, for we heard the constant booming of falling sand ahead. It was impossible to trace the channel, so we swung idly about with the current. Suddenly, we stopped. Our usual proceeding in such cases was to leap out and push the boat off. That night, fortunately, we were chilly, and did not fancy a midnight ducking. Each taking an oar, we thrust at the bar. The oars went down to the grip in quicksand. Had we leaped out as usual, there would have been two burials that night without the customary singing.

We rocked the boat without result. We were trapped; so we smoked awhile, thought about the matter, and decided to go to bed. In the morning we would fasten on our cork

MOONLIGHT ON THE MISSOURI BELOW THE YELLOWSTONE

20

belts and reach shore—perhaps. Having reached shore, we would find a stray skiff and go on. But the *Atom II* seemed booked for a long wait on that quicksand bar.

During the night a violent shaking of the boat awakened us. A heavy wind was blowing, and the prow of the boat was swinging about. It soon stopped with a chug. We stood up and rocked the boat vigorously. It broke loose again, and swung half-way around. Continuing this for a half-hour, we finally drifted into deep water.

The next day we passed Cannon Ball River, and reached Standing Rock Agency in the late evening. Sitting Bull is buried there. After a late supper, we went in search of his grave. We found it after much lighting of matches at headstones, in a weed-grown corner of the Agency burying-ground. A slab of wood, painted white, bears the following inscription in black: "In Memory of Sitting Bull. Died Dec. 15, 1890."

Perched upon the ill-kept grave, we smoked for an hour under the flying moon. A dog howled somewhere off in the gloomy waste.

That night the Erinnyes, in the form of a swarm of mosquitoes, attacked us lying in our boat. The weary Kid rolled and swore till dawn, when a light wind sprang up *astern*. We hoisted our sail, and for one whole day cruised merrily, making sixty miles by sunset. This took us to the town of Mobridge.

I was charmed with the novelty of driving our old enemy in harness. So, letting the Kid go to sleep forward under the sail, I cruised on into the night. The wind had fallen somewhat, but it kept the canvas filled. The crooning of the water, the rustling of the sail, the thin voices of bugs on shore, and the guttural song of the frogs, shocking the general quiet—these sounds only intensified the weird calm of the night. The sky was cloudless, and the moon shone so brightly that I wrote my day's notes by its glow.

The winking lights of Mobridge slowly dropped astern and faded into the glimmering mist.

Lonely seamen all the night
Sail astonished amid stars.

MEETING A STEAMBOAT IN MID-STREAM

The remembered lines gave me the divine itch for quoting verses. I did so, until the poor tired Kid swore drowsily in his sleep under the mast. The air was of that invigorating coolness that makes you think of cider in its sociable stage of incipient snappiness. Sleepy dogs bayed far away. Lone trees approached me, the motion seeming to belong to them rather than to me, and drifted slowly past—austere spectral figures. Somewhere about midnight I fell asleep and was awakened by a flapping sail and a groaning mast, to find myself sprawling over the wheel. The wind had changed; it was once more blowing up-stream, and a drizzling rain was driving through the gloom. During my sleep the boat had gone ashore. I moored her to a drift log, lowered sail, flung a tarp over us, and went to sleep again. And the morning came—blanketed with gray oozing fog. The greater part of that day we rowed on in the rain without a covering. In the evening we reached Forest City, an odd little old town, looking wistfully across stream at the youthful red

and white government buildings of the Cheyenne Agency.

Despite its name, this town is utterly tree-
less! I once knew a particularly awkward,
homely, and freckled young lady named
"Lily." The circumstance always seemed
grimly humorous to me, and I remembered it
as we strolled through the town that could n't
live up to its name.

We were ravenously hungry, and as soon as
possible we got our feet under the table of the
town's dingy restaurant. A long, lean man
came to take our orders. He was a walking
picture of that condition known to patent
medicine as "before taking." I looked for
the fat, cheerful person who should illustrate
the effect of eating at that place, but in vain.
When the lean man reappeared with the two
orders carefully tucked away in the palms of
his bony hands, I thought I grasped the eti-
ology of his thinness. It was indeed a frugal
repast. We took in the situation at a glance.

"Please consider us four hearty men, if you
will," I said kindly; "and bring two more
meals." The man obeyed. My *third* order,

THE MOUTH OF THE JAMES RIVER

it seems, met objections from the cook.   The
lean man, after a half audible colloquy with
the presiding spirit of the kitchen, reported
with a whipped expression that the house was
"all out of grub."   I regretted the matter
very much, as I had looked forward to a long,
unbroken series of meals that evening.

Setting out at moonrise, just after sunset,
we reached Pascal Island, fifteen miles below,
before sleep came upon us in a manner not to
be resisted.   All night coyotes yelped from the
hilltops about us, recounting their imme-
morial sorrows to the wandering moon—a sort
of Hecate worship.

At sunset of the fifth day from Bismarck,
we pulled in at Pierre.   Although I had never
been there before, Carthage was not more hospitable to storm-tossed Æneas than Pierre to
the weather-beaten crew of the *Atom*.   At a
reception given us by Mr. Doane Robinson,
secretary of the State Historical Society, I felt
again the warmth of the great heart of the
West.

During the first night out of Pierre, the Kid,
having stood his watch, called me at about

one o'clock. The moon was sailing high. I grasped the oars and fell to rowing with a resolute swing, meaning, in the shortest possible time, to wear off the disagreeable stupor incident to arising at that time of night. I had been rowing some time when I noted a tree on the bank near which the current ran. Still drowsy, I turned my head away and pulled with a will. After another spell of energetic rowing, I looked astern, expecting to see that tree at least a mile behind. There was no tree in sight, and yet I could see in that direction with sufficient clearness to discern the bulk of a tree if any were there.

"I am rowing to beat the devil!" thought I; "that tree is away around the bend already!" So I increased the speed and length of my stroke, and began to come out of my stupor. Some time later, I happened to look behind me. *The tree in question was about three hundred yards ahead of the boat!* I had been rowing upstream for at least a half-hour in a strenuous race with that tree! The Kid, aroused by my laughter, asked sleepily what in thunder tickled me. I told him I had merely thought

THE YANKTON LANDING IN THE OLD DAYS

of a funny story; whereat he mumbled some
unintelligible anathema, and lapsed again into
a snoring state.   But I claim the distinction
of being the only man on record who ever
raced a half-hour with a tree, and finished
three city blocks to the bad!

The next day we rounded the great loop, in
which the river makes a detour of thirty miles.
Having rowed the greater part of the day, we
found ourselves in the evening only two or
three miles from a point we had reached in the
morning.

In a drizzling rain we passed Brule Agency.
In the evening, soppy and chilled, we were
pulling past a tumble-down shanty built under
the bluffs, when a man stepped from the door
and hailed us.   We pulled in.   "You fellers
looks like you needed a drink of booze," said
the man as we stepped ashore.   "Well, I got it
for sale, and it ain't no harm to advertise!"

This strenuous liquor merchant bore about
him all the wretched marks of the stuff he
sold.

"Have your wife cook us two meals," said I,
"and I 'll deal with you."

"Jump in my boat," said he. I got in his skiff, wondering what his whim might mean. After several strokes of the oars, he pulled a flask from his pocket, took my coin and rowed back to shore. "Government license," he explained; "got to sell thirty feet from the bank." "Poor old Government," thought I; "they beat you wherever they deal with you!"

We went up to the wretched shanty, built of driftwood, and entered. The interior was a mêlée of washtubs, rickety chairs, babies, and flies. The woman of the house hung out a ragged smile upon her puckered mouth, etched at the lips with many thin lines of worry, and aped hospitality in a manner at once pathetic and ridiculous. A little girl, who looked fifty or five, according to how you observed her, dexterously dodged the drip from the cracks in the roof, as she backed away into a corner, from whence she regarded us with eyes already saddened with the ache of life.

After my many days and nights in the great open, fraternizing with the stars and

21

"ATOM II" LANDING AT SIOUX CITY

the moon and the sun and the river, it gave
me a heartache to have the old bitter human
fact thrust upon me again. "What is there
left here to live for?" thought I. And just
then I noted, hanging on the wall where the
water did not drip, a neatly framed marriage
certificate. This was the one attempt at
decoration.

It was the household's 'scutcheon of respec-
tability. This woman, even in her degrada-
tion, true to the noblest instinct of her sex,
clung to this holy record of a faded glory.

Two days later, pushing on in the starlit
night, we heard ahead the sullen boom of
waters in turmoil. For a half-hour, as we
proceeded, the sound increased, until it
seemed close under our prow. We knew
there was no cataract in the entire lower portion of the river; and yet, only from a waterfall had I ever heard a sound like that. We
pulled for the shore, and went to bed with
the sinister booming under our bow.

Waking in the gray of dawn, we found ourselves at the mouth of the Niobrara River.
Though a small stream compared with the

Missouri, so great is its speed, and so tremendous the impact of its flood, that the
mightier, but less impetuous Missouri is driven
back a quarter of a mile.

Reaching Springfield—twelve miles below—
before breakfast, in the evening we lifted
Yankton out of a cloud of flying sand. The
next day Vermilion and Elk Point dropped
behind; and then, thirty miles of the two
thousand remained.

In the weird hour just before the first faint
streak of dawn grows out of the dark, we were
making coffee—the last outdoor coffee of the
year. Oh, the ambrosial stuff!

We were under way when the stars paled.
At sunrise the smoke of Sioux City was waving
huge ragged arms of welcome out of the southeast. At noon we landed. We had rowed
fourteen hundred miles against almost continual head winds in a month, and we had
finished our two thousand miles in two months.
It was hard work. And yet——

The clang of the trolleys, the rumble of the
drays, the rushing of the people!

I prefer the drifting of the stars, the wandering of the moon, the coming and going of the sun, the crooning of the river, the shout of the big, manly, devil-may-care winds, the boom of the diving beaver in the night.

I never felt at home in a town. Up river when the night dropped over me, somehow I always felt comfortably, kindly housed. Towns, after all, are machines to facilitate getting psychically lost.

When I started for the head of navigation a friend asked me what I expected to find on the trip. "Some more of myself," I answered.

And, after all, that is the Great Discovery.

THE END